Emoji CROCHET

20 Easy-to-Make Projects Expressing Attitude & Style

Emoji CROCHET

20 Easy-to-Make Projects Expressing Attitude & Style

Charles Voth

SPRING HOUSE PRESS

THANKS
Many thanks to the crocheters who crocheted the following projects:
Fran Elsky: Big Grin Hoodie and Kissy Pocket Scarf
Andrea Giattini: 9 Faces Lapghan
Deb Seda-Testut: 25's a Crowd Blanket
Nancy Smith: Taunting Mega Cushion

Publisher: Paul McGahren
Editorial Director: Matthew Teague
Editor: Kerri Grzybicki
Design: Lindsay Hess
Layout: Michael Douglas
Project illustration: Charles Voth
Stitch illustration: Carolyn Mosher
Photography: Danielle Atkins
Technical Editor: Tian Connaughton

Spring House Press
3613 Brush Hill Court
Nashville, TN 37216
ISBN: 978-1-940611-72-3

Library of Congress Control Number: 2017941646
Printed in the United States of America
First Printing: July 2017

Thanks to the following companies for providing the yarns used to create the
samples shown in the photographs: Bernat, Caron, and Patons by Spinrite Yarns
(www.yarnspirations.com); Cascade Yarns (www.cascadeyarns.com); Handy Hands
(www.hhtatting.com); Kraemer Yarns (www.kraemeryarns.com); Universal Yarn
(www.universalyarn.com).

Note: The following list contains names used in *Emoji Crochet* that may be
registered with the United States Copyright Office: Bernat; Caron; Cascade Yarns; Craft Yarn
Council; Hacky Sack; Handy Hands; Kraemer Yarns; Patons; Spinrite Yarns; Universal Yarn.

To learn more about Spring House Press books, or to find a retailer near you,
email info@springhousepress.com or visit us at www.springhousepress.com.

ACKNOWLEDGEMENTS

To friends, colleagues, and teachers in the world of fiber, I owe many thanks. My deepest gratitude goes to my friend, Judith McCabe; Matthew Teague; my patient editor, Kerri Grzybicki; and the rest of the Spring House Press team, who have granted me the wondrous opportunity to share fun crochet with so many new people. To Fran Elsky and CGOA friends Andrea Giattini, Nancy Smith, and Deb Seda-Testut, your patience with my experimental ways, patterns in stages, and non-linear thinking ended up being very generous, and your crochet work for the models is impeccable! Vashti Braha, you encouraged me to return to the world of crochet, and I can't even begin to express the depth of my appreciation. To Mary Beth Temple, my business mentor and friend, thanks so much for the laughs, for trusting my ability, and for pushing me to get out there and to stay the course. To my sons, Zachary and Sebastian, you are the reason I pursue creativity, beauty, and fun, and to see you chase those same things makes me realize how worth it this journey has been. And to my wife Pam: you have believed in me like no other, encouraging my flights of fancy while keeping me tethered to reality, tethered to you. You are my hermitage, my dwelling forever, and my thankfulness knows no bounds.

CONTENTS

CLOTHES

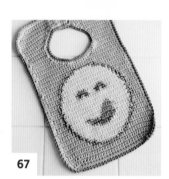

ACCESSORIES

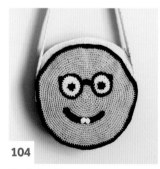

HOME DECOR

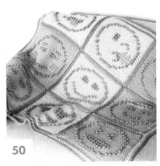

CROCHET STITCHES AND TECHNIQUES

Whether you are a pro at crocheting or completely new to the hobby, this section provides the basic stitches and techniques you need to know to succeed.

CROCHET STITCHES

Slipknot

1: Make a loop with the yarn, leaving a 6-inch tail, and pinch where it crosses itself. Lay this over the strand of yarn that leads to the ball of yarn (called the "working" yarn).

2: Insert the hook into the loop and under the strand of working yarn and lift it up through the loop. Gently pull on the tail to close the loop around the working yarn, which now forms the loop on the hook. This is called the "live" loop because if it comes off the hook, your crochet fabric will unravel.

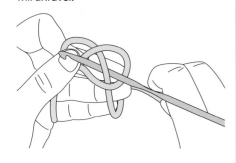

Yarn Over (YO)

Right-hand crocheters: Wrap the yarn over your hook from back to front; some will prefer to rotate the hook counter-clockwise to make the wrap.

Left-hand crocheters: Wrap the yarn over your hook from back to front; some will prefer to rotate the hook clockwise to make the wrap.

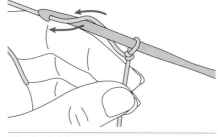

Chain (ch)

1: Make a slipknot on the hook.

2: Yarn over (YO) and pull the yarn through the loop on the hook. You will now have a loop on your hook, a chain stitch below the hook, and the slipknot below that first chain. Be sure the chains are loose enough that you can see a small space (about ⅓ of the width of the hook you are using) between the middle of a chain and the base of the next one.

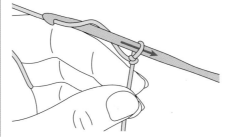

3: Repeat step 2 until you've crocheted the number of chains that were indicated in the pattern instructions. To count the chains, do not count the live loop nor the knot. Each V-shaped stitch between those two points is counted as a chain.

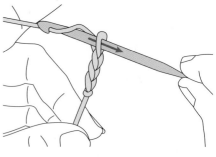

Slip Stitch (sl st)

Keep your tension comfortably loose to make this stitch. Insert the hook into the indicated stitch or space, yarn over, draw the strand of yarn through the insertion location and immediately through the loop on the hook.

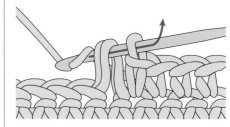

Single Crochet (sc)

1: Insert the hook into the indicated stitch, chain, or space and yarn over. Pull up the loop through the insertion point, giving you 2 loops on the hook.

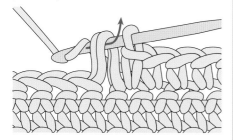

2: Yarn over and pull the strand through both loops on the hook to finish the single crochet.

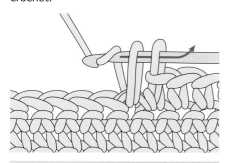

Half Double Crochet (hdc)

1: Wrap the yarn over the hook and insert the hook into the indicated stitch, chain, or space and yarn over again. Pull up the loop through the insertion point, giving you 3 loops on the hook.

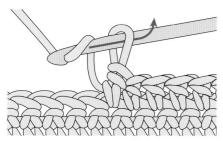

2: Yarn over and pull the strand through all 3 loops on the hook to finish the half double crochet.

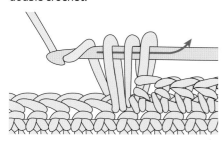

Double Crochet (dc)

1: Wrap the yarn over the hook and insert the hook into the indicated stitch, chain, or space and yarn over again. Pull up the loop through the insertion point, giving you 3 loops on the hook.

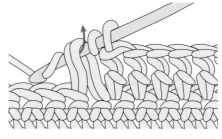

2: Yarn over and pull the strand through the first two loops on the hook.

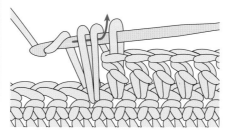

3: Repeat step 2 to finish the double crochet stitch.

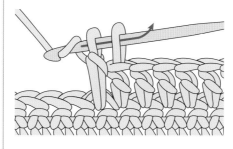

Treble Crochet (tr)

1: Wrap the yarn over the hook twice and insert the hook into the indicated stitch, chain, or space and yarn over again. Pull up the loop through the insertion point, giving you 4 loops on the hook.

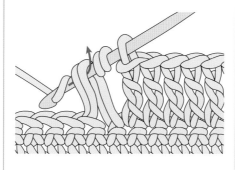

2: Yarn over and pull the strand through the first 2 loops on the hook.

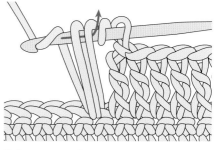

3: Repeat step 2.

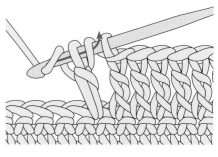

4: Repeat step 2 to finish the treble crochet stitch.

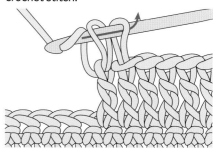

Post Stitches

Post stitches can cause stitches from previous rows to stand out towards the facing side of the fabric (called front posts) or to recede into the background (called back posts). Single, half double, double, and treble crochet stitches can all be made as post stitches. A post stitch is worked around the next indicated stitch by inserting the hook in and out of the fabric such that the post (or lower part) of the stitch worked around either recedes into the fabric or pushes out toward the crocheter.

For back post stitches (receding), insert the hook from the back of the fabric to the front in the gap before the post of the indicated stitch. Then, from the front, push the hook back through the fabric to the back in the gap after the indicated stitch. Yarn over and then pull back the strand through both sides of the indicated stitch and up to allow the rest of the stitch to be made.

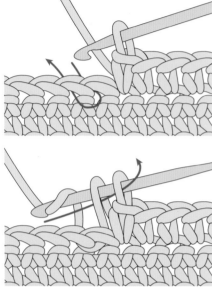

For front post stitches, insert the hook from the front to the back and then to the front again, beginning in the gap before the post of the indicated stitch around to the gap after the same post. Yarn over and complete the rest of the stitch.

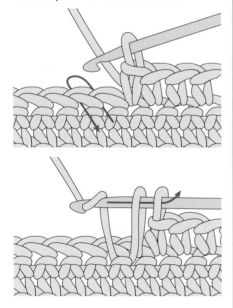

Skipping Stitches (sk)

As the pattern indicates, count the number of stitches and then proceed to work the next stitches in the next insertion point given in the instructions.

Two Single Crochet Decreases (sc2tog)

Version A

1: Insert hook in next stitch, yarn over, and pull up a loop.

2: Repeat step 1 in next stitch.

3: Yarn over and pull through all 3 loops on hook.

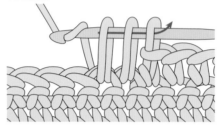

Version B

Some yarns leave more gaps than others, so this is an alternative to avoid gaps.

1: Insert hook in front loop only of next stitch.

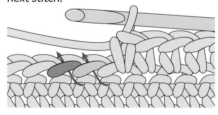

2: Repeat step 1 in next stitch.

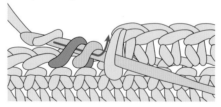

3: Yarn over and draw through all loops on hook.

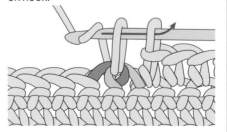

Tilted-A Stitch (t-A st)

1: Yarn over hook and insert hook under 2 loops of stitch at the base of current stitch.

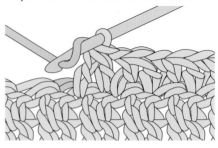

2: Yarn over hook and pull up loop.

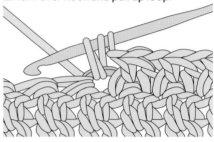

3: Yarn over hook and pull through the 2 loops; the first leg has been made.

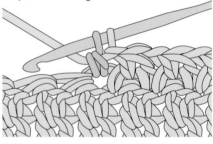

4: Yarn over hook and insert hook under 4 strands in the heart of the next stitch. The insertion point is shown here.

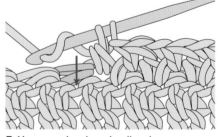

5: Yarn over hook and pull up loop.

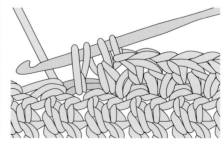

6: Yarn over and pull through the 2 loops; the 2nd leg has now been made.

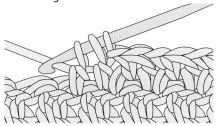

7: Yarn over and pull through all loops on hook.

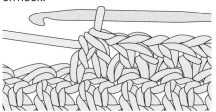

The completed tilted A stitch looks like a capital letter A.

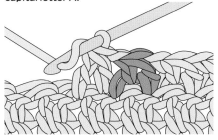

Foundation Single Crochet (fsc)

Chain stitch 3, insert hook in first chain stitch, yarn over, and pull up a loop, yarn over and pull through first loop on hook (this counts as base chain stitch), yarn over, pull through 2 loops on hook (first foundation single crochet made). *Insert hook into 2 strands of base chain stitch, yarn over, pull up loop, yarn over, pull through first loop on hook (base chain stitch made), yarn over, pull through 2 loops on hook; repeat from * the number of times indicated.

Foundation Double Crochet (fdc)

Chain stitch 3, insert hook in first chain stitch, yarn over, and pull up a loop, yarn over and pull through first loop on hook (this counts as base chain stitch), [yarn over, pull through 2 loops on hook] twice (first foundation double crochet made). *Insert hook into 2 strands of base chain stitch, yarn over, pull up loop, yarn over, pull through first loop on hook (base chain stitch made), [yarn over, pull through 2 loops on hook] twice; repeat from * the number of times indicated.

CROCHET TECHNIQUES

Where to Work Stitches

Each chain stitch has two strands that look like a braid or hearts. When the chain is held horizontally with the right side up, the strand closest to you is called the front loop and the strand facing away from you is the back loop. When working into a starting chain to work in back and forth rows, it is possible to insert the hook in one of the following three places. Choose the one you like best and stay consistent across the first row of stitches.

First, insert the hook under just the back loop and finish the stitch as instructed.

Second, insert the hook under the back loop together with the strand of yarn that is under it.

Third, flip the chain over to reveal a ridge on the back of each chain stitch. Insert the hook under each ridge to make a stitch. This is called working into the back bump, ridge, or bar.

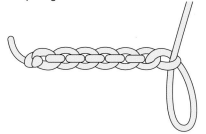

Once you are working into other stitches and not into chains, the hook should be inserted under both loops at the top of the stitches from the previous row. Only insert the hook differently if told to. Instructions may say to make a single crochet in the back loop only, in which case find the strand furthest from you and insert the hook under it. If the instructions say to insert the hook in the front loop only, insert the hook under the top strand that is closest to you. When you aren't supposed to work the top two usual strands for the whole row, instructions will be given at the beginning of the row or round explaining what to do for the entire row or round.

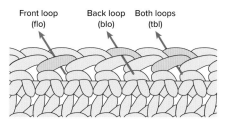

In some instances, stitches are skipped and replaced with a chain or a series of chain stitches that strand across the missed stitch(es), making a gap called a chain space. Unless indicated otherwise, on following rows or rounds, it is usual to insert the hook completely under the chain strand into that gap or "chain space" (ch-sp) and to finish the stitch you are making from that point.

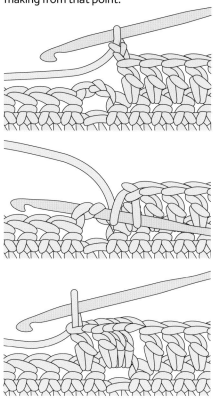

Working in Rows

Many patterns involve working across a row, then turning and continuing with the following row. Some instructions will ask you to make some chain stitches to bring the hook up to the same height of the stitches you are about to make across the new row; this is called a "turning chain" (tch).

In some cases, a turning chain will stand in for another stitch. This will be indicated as follows: Ch 3 (counts as first double crochet). In this case, the stitch at the base of the turning chain will be skipped and the next stitch should be considered the second stitch of the row. When working back on the following row, the turning chain that counts as a double crochet will be the last stitch to be worked into and you should be careful to crochet into that turning chain to get the correct number of stitches for that row. All exceptions should be stated in the pattern.

In some cases, turning chains will not count as the first stitch and will read as follows: "Ch 1, sc in first 2 sts." The initial ch 1 is the turning chain, but it is not counted as a stitch. When you work back toward the end of the following row, you would not crochet into that ch 1 in order to get the right stitch count.

Working in the Round

Some patterns are worked in a joined round. Work a slip stitch into the top of the first stitch of the round as instructed. You may or may not be asked to turn the work to go in the opposite direction. Some patterns are worked in a spiral round without a slip stitch join. At the end of the round, keep crocheting into the next round. Use a stitch marker to mark the beginning of the round.

Working into Both Sides of a Starting Chain

1: To crochet along both sides of a starting chain, start by inserting the hook under the back ridge loops of the chain and then rotate the work with the same side facing rather than turning to work back along the stitches just made.

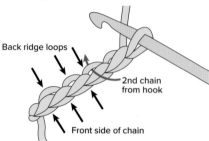

Back ridge loops

2nd chain from hook

Front side of chain

2: Crochet the indicated number of chain stitches given in the pattern instructions. Work the first stitch into the back ridge of the 2nd stitch from the hook. To find this first stitch easily, place a stitch marker in it. Crochet the remaining stitches as indicated to the end of the starting chain. In the last stitch next to the slip knot, there will usually be more than one stitch worked; follow the pattern. Rotate the piece 180 degrees to continue into the other side of the starting chain.

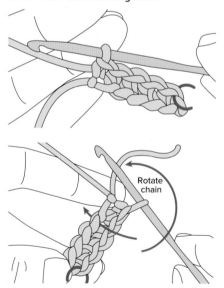

Rotate chain

3: Insert the hook under both strands at the top of each chain as you work across this side. When you reach the last stitch, the instructions will most likely have you increase there with more than one stitch. Then you will join to the first stitch (the

one with the marker) with a slip stitch or continue in a spiral fashion without joins.

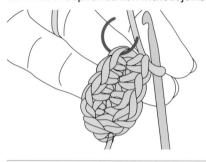

Adjustable Ring

This reduces the size of the hole in your starting round.

1: Make a ring with the yarn that has a 6-inch tail. As you would for a slip knot, put the hook in the loop.

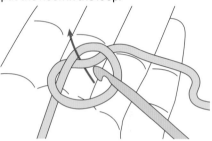

2: Yarn over the hook. Pull the yarn through the loop for a slip stitch, but don't tighten it.

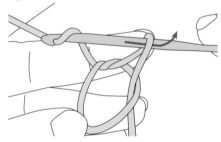

3: Chain 1 and, over both strands of yarn that make the adjustable ring, proceed to single crochet the number of times instructed. Pull the tail to close the ring.

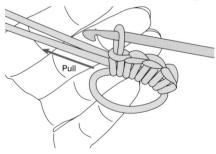

Pull

Make the next stitch of the next round in the first single crochet of the finished ring.

Right Side (RS) and Wrong Side (WS)

The side of the work that will eventually be the "public" side is called the right side of the work. Pattern instructions that involve rows or rounds being worked in both directions with turns and turning chains will indicate which rows or rounds are the right side of the work. It is not always the odd rows that are the right side of the work. The front loops and back loops of the top of the chain are relative to the person crocheting, not relative to the right or the wrong side of the work. When you are crocheting with the right side facing you, the front loops of the stitches are the ones nearest you, but if you turn the work, those loops now become the back loops of the stitches because they are furthest from you.

Changing Colors

To change colors, or to add a new ball of yarn in the same color, crochet to the place just before you make the last stitch with the current color. In the next stitch, make the indicated stitch to the point where there are 2 loops left on the hook (3 loops for half double crochet). Let go of (called "dropping") the strand of the current color; leaving a tail, yarn over with the new color and pull it through the last 2 loops on the hook. Gently tighten the loops with both tails and proceed to crochet following stitches with the new color. The tails, or "ends," will be hidden in the crochet fabric, or "woven in" after more of the fabric has been crocheted.

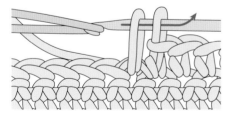

Knots in the Yarn

Do not crochet a knot into the fabric. Stop crocheting when there are 6 inches before the knot and cut as close as possible to both sides of the knot. Continue to join the yarn into the next stitch as if you were changing colors.

Sewn Invisible Join

1: Cut yarn, leaving a 4-inch tail, and pull end out of top of last stitch without tugging too hard.

2: Thread tail in tapestry needle; from wrong side to right side, insert needle under the two top loops of the 2nd stitch of the round.

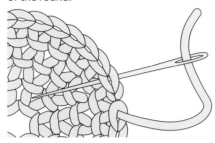

3: Pull until the stitch looks the same size as neighboring stitches. Insert the tapestry needle into the heart of the stitch from which the tail exits.

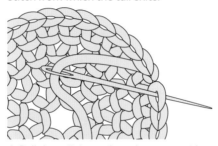

4: Pull the tail through to the wrong side of the work. Weave in the end under back strands of various stitches to secure tail before trimming close.

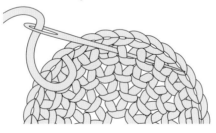

Puff Stitch

A puff stitch is a combination of half double crochet stitches that are all worked as a group into one insertion point. Puff stitches can be built out of 3, 4, or 5 stitches. The pattern will specify this number. Yarn over, insert hook in indicated stitch or space the number of times indicated, yarn over, and pull through all loops on hook. The illustration shows a 3-hdc puff stitch.

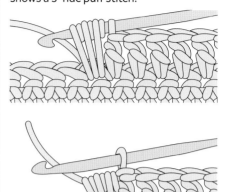

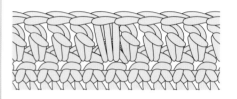

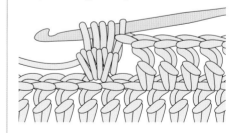

Clusters

Clusters come in two forms: bobble clusters and decreasing clusters. Bobble clusters are often simply called clusters and are worked into one insertion point. They typically are made of double crochet stitches, but it is possible to make them from treble crochet stitches or double-treble stitches. The pattern will define which stitches and how many to use. To make a bobble cluster with double crochet stitches:

1: Yarn over. Insert hook in indicated stitch. Yarn over. Pull up loop, yarn over, and pull through 2 loops on hook.

2: Repeat step 1 the number of times indicated (usually 3, but 2, 4, or more is also possible).

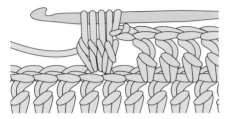

3: Yarn over and pull through all loops on the hook. The illustration shows a 4-dc bobble cluster (4dc-cl).

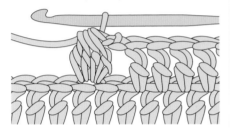

Decreasing clusters are worked in a similar way, but are worked into a series of insertion points usually, but not always, immediately next to each other. Decreasing clusters are labeled with the number used, the stitch used, and the word "together." In the illustration, you can see a dc4tog (double crochet 4 together). When this stitch is made, the hook goes into 4 different insertion points to make the bottom part of a double crochet. 4 stitches become 1 stitch, which is a decrease of 3 stitches. In some patterns, other chains or stitches are used to replace the missing 3 stitches, so the total number of stitches on a row or round does not decrease. Decreasing clusters are used both to create inverted triangle shapes and to actually decrease stitches; the pattern will explain the specifics for each situation.

1: To make a dc4tog, yarn over, insert hook in NEXT indicated stitch, and yarn over. Pull up loop, yarn over, pull through 2 loops on hook.

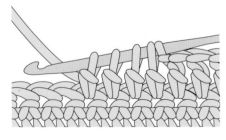

2: Repeat step 1 4 times; yarn over, and pull through all 5 loops on hook.

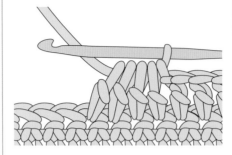

FINISHING STITCHES

Whip Stitch

This technique of sewing flat seams is one of the fastest. Line up the sides of the two pieces with their right sides together. With a tapestry needle and yarn, insert the needle from back to front through both layers of crocheted fabric and pull out on the side facing you. A short length further along the sides, re-insert the needle from the back through to the front of both layers and repeat across. Pull evenly and keep stitches tight as you work across. Normally, if you are working along sides that have the tops of the stitches visible, you can either work under all four strands of each pair of stitches, first under the two strands of the stitch on the back piece and then under the strands of the corresponding stitch on the front piece. This creates a small ridge on the inside of the seam. To lessen this ridge, insert the needle under the front loop only of the stitch on the rear piece of crocheted fabric and then under the back loop only of the corresponding stitch on the front piece of crochet.

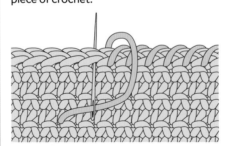

Mattress Stitch

This seaming technique produces a tight and almost invisible ridge that is very secure. Lay the two crocheted pieces to be seamed with right side up and their edges matching each other. Along the edges that you are joining, find an

insertion point (A) and an exit point (B) on the piece that is closest to you. Insert the tapestry needle threaded with yarn into A and out of B. Look for the corresponding segment of fabric—it may be a stitch, row, or section of a row on the opposite piece of crochet—and insert the needle into C and exit from D. The insertion point (C) and the exit point (D) are usually off-center from the corresponding points on the first piece of fabric rather than directly lined up with each other (see illustration).

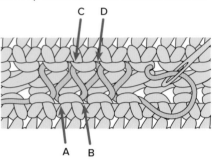

Cable Stitch

1: Insert needle through point A from behind.

2: With yarn below needle, insert at B and come out at C.

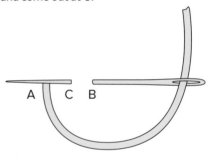

3: Keeping yarn above needle, insert at D and come through B.

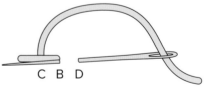

4: Repeat steps 2 and 3 to continue.

Double Running Stitch

1: Create a line of running stitches with the stitches and spaces all equal in length.

2: When you reach the end of the line, turn around and fill in the spaces by coming through from the back at A and inserting at B.

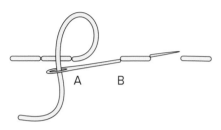

Satin Stitch

Apply satin stitches by grouping short- or medium-length stitches closely together to build up a shape or fill an area with color.

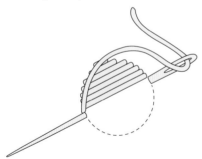

ADDING FACES TO YOUR PROJECTS

Depending on the project, there are a few ways presented for you to add faces to your emoji projects. Some pieces use separately crocheted facial features that then get sewn on; some items utilize embroidery stitches or pom-poms that you can arrange into any emoji face you like; and some projects have colored charts and instructions given to crochet the faces right into the project. Keep reading to find out which projects use what method.

CROCHETED FACIAL FEATURES

The following facial features can be crocheted and then sewn onto any fabric project you can think of. In this book, there are eight projects that use these crocheted facial features: 25's a Crowd Blanket (page 26), Stinky Feet Ottoman (page 32), Chillin' Out Cushion (page 36), Sweet Stuff Cushion (page 39), Baby Beanies (page 64), Surly Slouchie Hat (page 73), Kissy Pocket Scarf (page 80), and Brainiac Bag (page 104). Be sure to use the weight of yarn that matches the project you're working on so the scale of the facial features is correct.

Oval Eye, Small

Rnd 1: With black, work 7 sc in adjustable loop (magic ring), sl st in first sc to join. (7 sc)

Rnd 2: Ch 1, 2 sc in each st around, sl st in first sc to join. (14 sc)

Rnd 3: Ch 1, 1 sc, 1 hdc, 2dc in next st, 1 hdc, 10 sc, sl st in first sc to join. (15 sts) Fasten off.

Oval Eye, Medium

Work rnds 1 and 2 as for Oval Eye, Small.

Rnd 3: Ch 1, 1 sc, 1 hdc, 2dc in next st, 1 hdc, 10 sc, do not join, continue around in the next sts, 3 sc, 2sc in next st, 3 sc, 2sc in next st, 4 sc, sl st in next st. (17 sts) Fasten off.

Oval Eye, Large

Work rnds 1 and 2 as for Oval Eye, Small.

Rnd 3: Ch 1, 1 sc, 1 hdc, 2dc in next st, 1 hdc, 10 sc, do not join, continue around in the next sts, 4 sc, 2sc in next st, 1 sc, 2sc in next st, 1 sc, 2sc in next st, 2 sc, 2sc in next st, 2 sc, sl st in next st. (19 sts) Fasten off.

True Circle Eye, Small

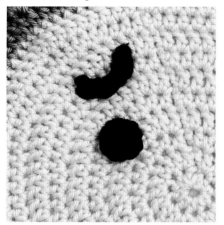

Work rnds 1 and 2 as for Oval Eye, Small. (14 sts) Fasten off.

True Circle Eye, Medium

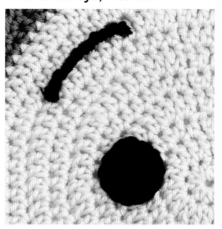

Work rnds 1 and 2 as for Oval Eye, Small.

Rnd 3: Ch 1, [1 sc, 2sc in next st] 7 times, sl st in first sc to join. (21 sts) Fasten off.

Squinting Eye

Row 1: With black, ch 18, hdc in back ridge of 2nd ch from hook, 5 hdc, 1 sc, 1 sl st, sk next ch, 1 sl st, 1 sc, 5 hdc, (1 hdc, 1 sc) in last ch. Fasten off.

Side-Looking Eye 1

This eye has a line that extends to the right.

Work rnds 1 and 2 as for Oval Eye, Small.

Rnd 3: Ch 1, [1 sc, 2 sc in next st] 6 times, 1 hdc, 1 fdc in next st, 3 fdc in base of each prev st, hdc in bottom of last fdc made. Fasten off.

Side-Looking Eye 2

This eye has a line that extends to the left.

Work rnds 1 and 2 as for Oval Eye, Small.

Rnd 3: Ch 1, [1 sc, 2sc in next st] 5 times, ch 5, turn.

Rnd 4: Hdc in 2nd ch from hook, dc in each of next 3 chs, yo, insert hook in flo of same st as dc just made, yo, pull up lp, yo, pull through 2 lps on hook, sk 1 st, insert hook in next st, yo, pull up lp, yo, pull through all lps on hook, sc in each of next 3 sts. Fasten off.

X Over Eyes

Rnd 1: With black, ch 11, [*sl st in back ridge of 2nd ch from hook, sl st in each of next 4 chs*, ch 6], rep btwn [ ] once, rep btwn * * once, sl st in back ridge of each of first 5 chs. Fasten off.

Hearts, Small

Rnd 1: With pink, work 7 sc in adjustable loop (magic ring), sl st in first sc to join. (7 sc)

Rnd 2: Ch 3 (counts as first dc), 2 dc in st at base of ch-3 just made, 1 hdc, 1 sc, (1 sc, 1 hdc, 1 sc) in next st (heart point made), 1 sc, 1 hdc, (2 dc, ch 3, sl st) in next st, sl st in next sl st. (14 sts)

Rnd 3: In each st around work in blo as follows: sc to top of first bump, 2sc in next st, 2sc in each st to heart point, work (1 sc, ch 1, sl st) in middle hdc, sc in each st to top of 2nd bump, 2 sc in next st, sc in last sts, sl st in sl st from prev rnd. (18 sts) Fasten off.

Closed Eye, Small

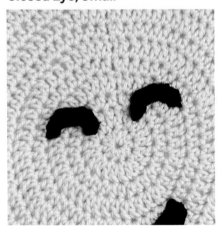

Row 1: With black, ch 13, sc in back ridge of 2nd ch from hook, [sk next ch, sc in back ridge of next ch] 5 times, sc in last ch. Fasten off.

Hearts, Medium

Work rnds 1 and 2 as for Hearts, Small.

Rnd 3: Sc in first and 2nd ch of beg ch-3 from prev rnd, 2 sc in 3rd ch, 2sc in next dc, sc in each of next 5 sts, ch 2, sl st in back ridge of 2nd ch from hook, sc in same st as last sc worked, sc in each of next 4 sts, 2sc in each of next 2 sts, sl st in sl st from prev rnd. (24 sts)

Rnd 4: 1 sc in next st, 2sc in each of next 2 sts, 3 sc, 2sc in next st, 5 sc, sl st in blo of next st, 3 sc, 2sc in next st, 3 sc, 2sc in each of next 2 sts, sl st in next st. (29 sts) Fasten off.

Closed Eye, Large

Row 1: With black, ch 14, sc in back ridge of 2nd ch from hook, sc in black ridge of each of next 11 chs, 2 sc in last ch, rotate work 180 degrees with same side facing.

Row 2: Working into other lp of beginning ch, [1 sc, sc2tog] twice, [sc2tog, 1 sc] twice, 1 sc in same st as last sc. Fasten off.

Round Eye with Pupil

Cut 1 yard (1m) of pearl white and set aside.

Make 2.

Rnd 1: With navy blue, make 8 hdc in adjustable ring, changing to pearl in last yo, and pull through 8th hdc, sl st in first hdc to join. (8 hdc)

Rnd 2: Ch 1, [1 sc, 2sc in next st] 4 times, sl st in first hdc to join, place lp on hook on sm. (12 sts)

Rnd 3: Sk next 3 sts, join 1 yard (1m) of pearl white in next st with sl st, ch 1, sc in same st as join, sc in next 2 sts, fasten off. Return lp on sm to hook, working into regular sts and the extra added sts: [1 sc in next st, 2sc in next st] around, join in first sc. (18 sc)

Rnd 4: Ch 1, [2 sc, 2sc in next st] around, changing to navy blue in last st, join in first sc. (24 sc)

Rnd 5: With navy blue, [2 sc, 2sc in next st] 6 times, sc in rem sts, join in first sc. (30 sts) Fasten off.

Eye with Off-Center Pupil

Make 2.

Rnd 1: With black, 6 sc in adjustable ring, join in first sc. (6 sc)

Rnd 2: Ch 1, 2 sc in each st around, join in first sc. (12 sc) Fasten off.

Rnd 3: With white, join in any st, ch 1, sc in same st as join, [2sc in next st, sc in next st] twice, 2sc in next st, 2hdc in next st, 2dc in next st, (dc, hdc) in next st, (hdc, sc) in next st, sc in next st, 2sc in next st, sl st in first sc to join. (20 sts)

Rnd 4: Ch 1, 2sc in same st as join, 2sc in next st, 2 sc, 2sc in next st, 4 sc, 2hdc in next st, 2dc in each of next 2 sts, 2hdc in each of next 2 sts, 4 sc, 2sc in next st, 1 sc in last st, join in first st. (29 sts) Fasten off.

Rnd 5: With black, join in any st, ch 1, sc in same st as join, 13 sc, sc in next st, 3 sc, 2sc in next st, 10 sc, join in first st. Fasten off.

Sunglasses, First Lens

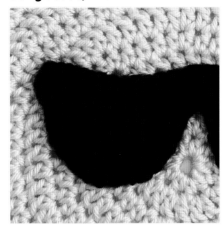

Row 1: With black, work 4 sc in adjustable loop (magic ring), turn. (4 sc)

Row 2: Ch 1, 2sc in each st, turn. (8 sc)

Row 3: Ch 1, [1 sc, 2sc in next st] 4 times, turn. (12 sc)

Row 4: Ch 1, [2 sc, 2sc in next st] 4 times, turn. (16 sc) Fasten off.

Eyes with Spectacles

Follow instructions for Round Eye with Pupil.

Earpieces: Lay eyes beside each other. Referring to picture, starting in 3 or 4 sts before (and after for other eye) top st of frame, join, ch 1, hdc in next st, ch 1, sl st in next st. Fasten off. You may need to play around with placement of these until they are symmetrical.

Nose piece: With navy blue, ch 4, (sc, hdc) in 2nd ch from hook, 2 hdc in next ch, (hdc, sc) in last ch. Fasten off.

Sunglasses, 2nd Lens and Frames

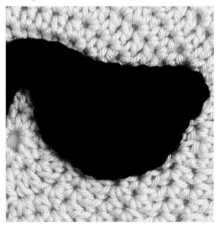

Work rows 1–4 as for First Lens.

Row 5: Ch 1, 9 sc evenly across flat side of lens, ch 2, 10 sc evenly across flat side of first lens, rotate piece to work around curves with same side facing, ch 1, sc in first st, [2sc in next st, 3 sc] 3 times, sc in last 2 sts, sc in back of each ch, sc in st in next lens, [2sc in next st, 3 sc] 3 times, sc in last 2 sts, ch 2, sl st in 2nd ch from hook, ch 1, sc in each st across flat tops of lenses to last st, 2sc in last st, ch 2, sl st in 2nd ch from hook, sl st in next st around lens. Fasten off.

Eyebrows

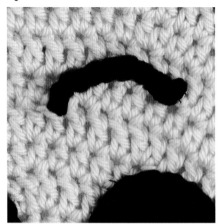

Use Closed Eye, Small or ch desired length, sl st in back ridge of 2nd ch from hook and in each rem ch.

Eyebrows, Straight

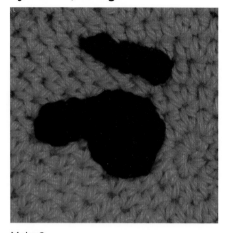

Make 2.

With black, ch 7, sc in 2nd ch, sc in next 4 sts, (sc, ch 1, sl st) in last ch. Fasten off.

Wide Grin

With black, work First Lens of Sunglasses.

Rnd 5: Ch 1, 9 sc evenly across flat side of lens, ch 2, sl st in 2nd ch from hook, rotate piece to continue around curve, 2sc in first st, [3 sc, 2sc in next st] 4 times, sl st in side of next st, turn, ch 2, sk sl st just made, sl st in each of next 2 sts.

Moustache

Row 1: With black, ch 27, sl st in blo of 2nd ch from hook, sl st in blo of each of next 4 chs, 2 sc, 2 hdc, 2 ldc (see page 39), 1 linked tr, ch 1, sl st 3 times alongside tr just made, sl st in next 2 chs, ch 3, linked tr in same ch, linked tr in next ch, 2 hdc, 2 sc, sl st in blo of next 5 chs, ch 1, rotate work 180 degrees. (25 sts)

Row 2: Working in opposite side of starting chs, sl st in next 5 sts, 2 sc, sl st in next 5 sts, sk next st, sl st in next 5 sts, 2 sc, sl st in each rem st. Fasten off.

Lipstick

Row 1: With red, ch 15, sc in 2nd ch from hook, 1 hdc, 3 dc, 1 hdc, 2 sc, 1 hdc, 3 dc, 1 hdc, (1 sc, sl st, 1 sc) in last ch, rotate work 180 degrees. (16 sts)

Row 2: Working in opposite side of starting chs, 1 hdc, 10 dc, 1 hdc, 1 sc, sl st in side of first sc. Fasten off.

Short Curved Mouth

Work as for Larger Closed Eye.

Straight Mouth

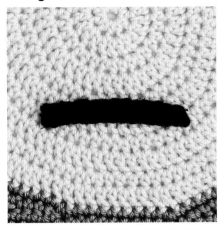

Row 1: With black, ch 21, hdc in 2nd ch from hook, hdc in each ch across to last ch, (hdc, sc) in last ch, rotate 180 degrees. (21 sts)

Row 2: Sc across opposite side of starting chs in each ch, sl st in side of first hdc. Fasten off.

Mouth, Large

Row 1: With black, ch 23, sc in 2nd ch from hook, 2 sc, [sc2tog, sc] 6 times, 2 sc, 3sc in last ch, rotate work 180 degrees. (18 sts)

Row 2: Working in opposite side of starting chs, sc in each st across, sl st in side of first sc. Fasten off.

Mouth, Extra-Large

With blue, ch 30, dc in 4th ch from hook, dc in next ch, [dc2tog, 2 dc] 6 times, (dc, ch 2, sl st) in last ch. Fasten off.

Smoochy Lips, Small

Row 1: With black, ch 15, sl st in blo in 2nd ch from hook, 2 sl st in blo, sk 1 ch, 2 sl st in blo, (1 sc, 1 sl st) in next ch, 3 sl st in blo, sk 1 ch, 3 sl st in blo. Fasten off.

Smoochy Lips, Large

Row 1: With black, ch 18, sc in back ridge of 2nd ch from hook, working in back ridges, 2 sc, 3sc in next ch, 3 sc, sk 1 ch, sc2tog, 2 sc, 3sc in next ch, 4 sc. (19 sts) Fasten off.

Grimacing Lips

With black, ch 22, sl st in blo of 2nd ch from hook, 2 sl st in blo, sk 1 ch, 2 sl st in blo, *(1 sc, 1 sl st) in next ch, 3 sl st in blo, sk 1 ch, 2 sl st in blo;* rep btwn * *, 1 sl st in blo. Fasten off.

Holding Breath Mouth

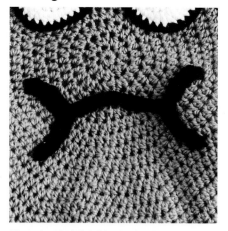

First cheek: With black, ch 13, 2 sc in 2nd ch from hook, sc in next ch, [2sc in next ch, sc in next 2 chs] twice, [2sc in next ch, sc in next ch] twice, turn. (17 sc)

Bottom lip and 2nd cheek: Sl st in first 8 sc, ch 24, sc in 2nd ch from hook, [sc2tog, sc in next st] twice, sc2tog, do not turn.

2nd cheek and top lip: Ch 8, sc in 2nd ch from hook, sc in next ch, [sc in next ch, 2sc in next ch] twice, sc in next ch, sc in opposite side of each of next 14 lip sts, sl st to first ch. Fasten off.

Tongue

Rnd 1: With pink, ch 9, (3 dc, 1 hdc) in 3rd ch from hook, sc in each of next 5 chs, 3sc in last ch, rotate work, working in opposite side of chs, 8 sc. (20 sts)

Rnd 2: Sc in first dc, 2sc in each of next 3 sts, 6 sc, 3sc in next st, 9 sc, [2sc in next st, 1 sc] 3 times, 4 sc, sl st in next st. Fasten off.

Tears or Beads of Sweat

Rnd 1: With blue, work ch 2 (counts as first hdc), 6 hdc into adjustable loop (magic ring), sl st to join in top of beg ch-2. (7 hdc)

Rnd 2: Ch 1, sc in same st as join, 2sc in next st, 2 sc in next st, 1 sc, 2sc in next st, sc in next st, ch 2, sl st in 2nd ch from hook, sl st in side of last sc made, sl st in top of first sc. Fasten off.

Rosy Cheeks

With pink, make Small True Circle eyes.

Teeth

Make 2.

With pearl white, ch 3, sl st in 2nd and 3rd chs from hook, rotate work 180 degrees, tucking knot under, sl st in opposite side of next 2 starting ch. Fasten off.

Horns

Make 2.

Rnd 1: With orange and size E/4 (3.75mm) hook, 4 sc in adjustable ring, do not join, continue to work as a spiral.

Rnd 2: 1 sc, 2sc in next st, 2 sc. (5 sc)

Rnd 3: 2 sc, 2sc in next st, 2 sc. (6 sc)

Rnd 4: 1 sc, 2sc in each of next 4 sts, 1 sc. (10 sc)

Rnd 5: 2 sc, 2sc in next st, 1 sc, 2sc in each of next 2 sts, 1 sc, 2sc in next st, 2 sc. (14 sc)

Rnd 6: 14 sc, sl st in next st. Fasten off.

EMBROIDERING FACIAL FEATURES

Some projects have embroidered facial features. You can make the face shown in the photos, or create your own. Use a double running stitch (page 15) to make an outline around the shape you choose to include. To fill the shape, use long and short satin stitches (page 15). These consist of lines that are tightly placed parallel to each other to fill in the gap. The insertion and exit points of the tapestry needle do not have to line up; in fact, staggering them is better and gives a more solid look to the shape. Then, create the facial features using a cable stitch or double running stitch (page 15). The following projects are made with this method: Not Too Blue for You Mittens (page 83) and Smelly Slippers (page 87).

POM-POM FACIAL FEATURES

For Pom-Pom Beanie (page 76), you will create the face by attaching pom-poms in the desired shape.

EMOJIS CROCHETED INTO PROJECTS

Many of the projects in this book feature emoji faces that are crocheted right into the pattern following either text or a visual chart. Follow the instructions given with each project for this type. More information about the types of crochet stitches used can be found in the section starting on page 8. Projects that use this method are: Taunting Mega Cushion (page 42), 9 Faces Lapghan (page 50), Num Num Bib (page 67), Big Grin Hoodie (page 90), Bobble Head Earrings (page 107), Sleepy Time Washcloth (page 110), Striped Pencil Case (page 116), and Cool Guy Hacky Sack (page 119).

HOME DECOR

This chapter is overflowing with fun projects to deck out your personal space. Pillows, cushions, blankets, and even an ottoman are included. If you need a big blanket, check out the 25's a Crowd Blanket (page 26). For a smaller option, try the 9 Faces Lapghan (page 50). There are two normal-sized pillows to choose from—Chillin' Out Cushion (page 36) and Sweet Stuff Cushion (page 39)—or go big with the 30-inch (76cm) Taunting Mega Cushion (page 42). Lastly, don't forget a place to put your feet up with the Stinky Feet Ottoman (page 32).

25'S A CROWD BLANKET

With emoji friends, three is hardly enough to make a crowd. Crochet this blanket with as many faces as you want, and brighten up the room or couch of someone you love. The emoji facial elements from page 16 can be used in any combination to create 25 emoji faces, or if you want to add more squares to make a twin- or queen-sized blanket, you will have enough options to make each square unique!

FINISHED MEASUREMENTS
46 inches (1.17 m) square

GAUGE
First 4 rounds = 3 inches (7.5cm)

MATERIALS + TOOLS

- DK weight yarn (100% acrylic), 3.5 oz (100g) / 220 yds (200m) in the following colors:
  - 7 balls, yellow
  - 2 balls, black
  - 1 ball, pink
  - 1 ball, red
  - 2 balls, blue
  - 1 ball, green
  - 1 ball, pink-purple
  - 1 ball, violet
  - 1 ball, teal
- 4mm hook or size needed to achieve gauge
- Sharp tapestry needle

FACIAL FEATURES DIRECTORY

Note: The row is given as the first number, and the column as the second. The faces are presented as they appear on the photographed blanket from top left to bottom right.

Use the facial elements from Crocheted Facial Features (page 16) to customize your emoji design. Just be sure to use yarn that is the same weight as the rest of your project to keep the face proportional.

Position: 1-1
Border Color: Pink-Purple
Eyes: Side-Looking Eye 2
Mouth: Moustache
Other: Eyebrows

Position: 1-2
Border Color: Violet
Eyes: Squinting Eye
Mouth: Mouth, Large
Other: Rosy Cheeks

Position: 1-3
Border Color: Green
Eyes: Closed Eye, Small
Mouth: Mouth, Large
Other: Eyebrows

Position: 1-4
Border Color: Blue
Eyes: Oval Eye, Medium
Mouth: Wide Grin
Other: Tongue

Position: 1-5
Border Color: Teal
Eyes: Side-Looking Eye 1
Mouth: Small Mouth

Position: 2-1
Border Color: Green
Eyes: Closed Eye, Small
Mouth: Short Curved Mouth
Other: Rosy Cheeks

Position: 2-2
Border Color: Red
Eyes: Oval Eye, Medium
Mouth: Smoochy Lips, Small
Other: Eyebrows

Position: 2-3
Border Color: Blue
Eyes: Oval Eye, Large
Mouth: Oval Eye, Large
Other: Eyebrows

Position: 2-4
Border Color: Pink-purple
Eyes: Oval Eye, Large
Mouth: Mouth, Large

FACIAL FEATURES DIRECTORY, continued

Position: 2-5
Border Color: Violet
Eyes: Squinting Eye
Mouth: Wide Grin

Position: 3-1
Border Color: Red
Eyes: Closed Eye, Small
Mouth: Short Curved Mouth
Other: Tongue

Position: 3-2
Border Color: Green
Eyes: Closed Eye, Small
Mouth: Straight Mouth
Other: Eyebrows

Position: 3-3
Border Color: Violet
Eyes: Closed Eye, Small
Mouth: Lipstick

Position: 3-4
Border Color: Blue
Eyes: Oval Eye, Medium
Mouth: Small Mouth

Position: 3-5
Border Color: Teal
Eyes: Oval Eye, Small
Mouth: Oval Eye, Medium
Other: Eyebrows; Tears or Beads of Sweat

Position: 4-1
Border Color: Teal
Eyes: True Circle Eye, Medium
Mouth: Grimacing Lips
Other: Eyebrows

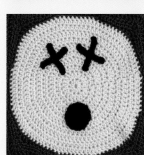

Position: 4-2
Border Color: Pink-purple
Eyes: X Over Eyes
Mouth: Oval Eye, Medium

Position: 4-3
Border Color: Green
Eyes: Sunglasses, First Lens; Sunglasses, 2nd Lens and Frames
Mouth: Mouth, Large

Position: 4-4
Border Color: Violet
Eyes: Side-Looking Eye 1; Side-Looking Eye 2
Mouth: Mouth, Large
Other: Eyebrows

FACIAL FEATURES DIRECTORY, continued

Position: 4-5
Border Color: Red
Eyes: Squinting Eye
Mouth: Mouth, Large
Other: Tongue

Position: 5-1
Border Color: Red
Eyes: Hearts, Small
Mouth: Short Curved Mouth

Position: 5-2
Border Color: Green
Eyes: True Circle Eye, Small
Mouth: Mouth, Large
Other: Closed Eye, Small

Position: 5-3
Border Color: Teal
Eyes: Closed Eye, Large
Mouth: Wide Grin
Other: Tears or Beads of Sweat

Position: 5-4
Border Color: Pink-purple
Eyes: Oval Eye, Small; Closed Eye, Small
Mouth: Mouth, Large

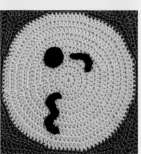

Position: 5-5
Border Color: Blue
Eyes: True Circle Eye, Medium; Closed Eye, Small
Mouth: Smoochy Lips, Large

YELLOW FACE

Note: You will need 25 yellow faces.

Rnd 1: With yellow, make an adjustable ring and ch 1, work 10 hdc into ring, sl st in top of first hdc to join. (10 hdc)

Rnd 2: Ch 2 (does not count as st here and throughout), 2 dc in each hdc around, sl st in top of first dc to join. (20 dc)

Rnd 3: Ch 2, [hdc in next st, 2hdc in next st] around, sl st in top of first hdc to join. (30 hdc)

Rnd 4: Ch 2, 2dc in each of first 2 sts, dc in next st, [2dc in next st, dc in next 2 sts]

around, sl st in top of first dc to join. (41 dc)

Rnd 5: Ch 2, [hdc in next st, 2hdc in next st, hdc in next 2 sts] 10 times, hdc in each rem st around, sl st in top of first hdc to join. (51 hdc)

Rnd 6: Ch 2, 2dc in each of first 2 sts, [dc in next 4 sts, 2dc in next st] 9 times, dc in each rem st around, sl st in top of first dc to join. (62 dc)

Rnd 7: Ch 2, [hdc in next 5 sts, 2hdc in next st] 10 times, hdc in each rem st around, sl st in top of first hdc to join. (72 hdc)

Rnd 8: Ch 2, 2dc in each of first 2 sts,

[dc in next 6 sts, 2dc in next st] 9 times, dc in each rem st around, sl st in top of first dc to join. (83 dc)

Rnd 9: Ch 2, hdc in next 3 sts, 2hdc in each of next 2 sts, [hdc in next 7 sts, 2hdc in next st] 9 times, hdc in each rem st around, sl st in top of first hdc to join. (94 hdc)

Rnd 10: Ch 2, [dc in next 8 sts, 2dc in next st] 10 times, dc in each rem st around, sl st in top of first dc. (104 dc)

Work sewn invisible join (see page 13). Weave in ends.

Rnd 11: In this step, you are completing the square around the face. In the photographed project, there are 5 faces with green, and 4 faces in each of these colors: blue, red, pink-purple, violet, and teal. With contrasting color according to detail images (page 28), a few stitches away from sewn invisible join, sl st loosely to join, ch 1, sc in same st, with darning needle, pull extra loose end through front and it will fall to the WS, *sc in next 5 sts, hdc in next 2 sts, dc in next 2 sts, hdc in next 2 sts, sc in next 6 sts, turn, leaving rem sts unworked, ch 1, sk first st, sc in next 3 sts, hdc in next 4 sts, [2 dc in next st] twice, hdc in next 4 sts, sc in next 2 sts, sl st in next st, turn, leaving rem sts unworked, sk sl st just made, sc in next 3 sts, hdc in next 3 sts, dc in next st, 2 dc in next st, ch 1, 2 dc in next st, dc in next st, hdc in next 3 sts, sc in next 4 sts, 1 sc in end of short row, 1 sc in same st as last one worked on rnd 10, sc in next 8 sts**, 2 sc in next st; rep from * around, ending final rep at **, sl st in first sc to join.

Rnd 12: Ch 2, dc in first 11 sts, [(dc, ch 1, dc) in corner ch-sp, 35 dc evenly across next side of square] 3 times, (dc, ch 1, dc) in 4th corner ch-sp, 24 dc evenly across to beg of rnd, sl st in top of first dc to join. (148 dc, 4 corner ch-1 sps)

Rnd 13: Ch 1, sc in same st as join, [sc in each st to next corner, 2sc in corner ch sp] 3 times, sc in each st to end of round.

Work sewn invisible join. Weave in ends.

FACIAL FEATURES

Create faces using the Facial Features instructions starting on page 16. Mix and match as desired. If you wish to create the faces shown in the photographed project, consult the grid on page 28. Referring to the photographs or according to your own preferences, with sewing thread and needle, attach facial features to project.

ASSEMBLY

Sew squares to each other with locking mattress stitch technique (see page 14).

BORDER

Rnd 1: With blue, join in any corner, ch 1, *3hdc in corner st, work 41 hdc evenly across side of each square and 1 hdc in seam to next corner*; rep btwn * * around, in last st change to black, sl st to first hdc.

Rnd 2: Ch 1, 1 sc, *3sc in corner, sc in each st to next corner*; rep btwn * * around, change to blue in last st, sl st to first.

Rnd 3: Ch 1, 2 sc, *3sc in corner, sc in each st to next corner*; rep btwn * * around, sl st to first st. Fasten off.

STINKY FEET OTTOMAN

Pouf cushions are great for sitting on, leaning against, or propping up your feet. That last option is what made me think of an emoji that's feeling a little nauseous from the smelly feet on top of him. With a color change and using emoji facial elements from page 16, you can give this comfy emoji pouf a whole new personality!

FINISHED MEASUREMENTS
26 inches (66cm) wide by 14 inches (36cm) high

GAUGE
With 6mm hook, 19 hdc = 6 inches (15cm)

MATERIALS + TOOLS

- Bulky weight yarn (100% acrylic), 3.5 oz (100g) / 148 yds (136m) per ball, in the following colors:
  - 9 balls, light green
  - 3 balls, black
  - 1 ball, white
- 6.5mm hook or size needed to achieve gauge
- 6mm hook or size needed to achieve gauge
- Stitch markers, 8
- Sharp tapestry needle
- 2½ yds (2.3m) fabric for lining, 30-in. (76cm) wide
- Sewing needle
- Matching green and black thread
- Foam peanuts or other beanbag-type filling

SPECIAL STITCHES

Place stitch marker (sm): Place sm in indicated st; on following rounds, move sm to 2nd (or only, depending on rnd) st worked into previously marked st.

Note: Join with sl st unless otherwise indicated.

FACIAL FEATURES DIRECTORY

Use the facial elements from Crocheted Facial Features (page 16) to customize your emoji design. Just be sure to use yarn that is the same weight as the rest of your project to keep the face proportional.

Eyes: Eye with Off-Center Pupil
Mouth: Holding Breath Mouth
Other: Closed Eye, Small

BASE

Rnd 1: With 6.5mm hook and green, form adjustable ring and make 7 sc in ring, join in first sc. (7 sc)

Rnd 2: Ch 1, 2 hdc in same st as join, 2 hdc in each st around, join in first hdc. (14 hdc)

Rnd 3: Ch 1, hdc in same st as join, dc in next st, 2hdc in next st, [(dc, hdc) in next st, (hdc, dc) in next st, 2hdc in next st] twice, (dc, hdc) in next st, hdc in next st, (dc, hdc) in next st, hdc in next st, dc in next st, hdc in last st, join in first hdc. (8 dc, 16 hdc)

Rnd 4: Ch 1, 2 hdc in same st as join, *fpdc around next dc, hdc in next st**, 2hdc in next st; rep from * around, ending final rep at **, join in first st. (32 sts)

Rnd 5: Ch 1, 2 hdc in same st as join, *1 hdc, fpdc around next st, 1 hdc**, 2hdc in next st; rep from * around, ending final rep at **, join in first hdc. (40 sts)

Rnd 6: Ch 1, 1 hdc in same st as join, 1 hdc, place sm (see Special Stitches) in st just made, 2hdc in next st, *fpdc around next st, 2hdc in next st*, 2 hdc, place sm in st just made, 2hdc in next st; rep from * around, ending final rep at **, join in first hdc. (56 sts)

Rnd 7: Ch 1, 1 hdc in same st as join, *hdc in each st across to marked st, 2hdc in marked st, move sm to 2nd hdc just made, hdc in each st across to next dc, fpdc around next dc; rep from * around, ending with hdc to last st, join in first st. (64 sts)

Rnd 8: Rep rnd 7. (72 sts)

Rnd 9: Ch 1, 1 hdc in same st as join, *hdc in each st across to 1 st before next dc, 2hdc in next st, fpdc around next dc, 2hdc in next st; rep from * around, ending with hdc in each st across to end of rnd, join in first st. (88 sts)

Rnds 10–24: Rep rnds 7–9. (248 sts)

Rnd 25: Ch 1, hdc in each st around.

SIDES

Rnd 26: With RS facing, look over the top edge of the sts to find the lower back bar from the WS of the hdc sts and work all sts in that strand this rnd as follows: Ch 1, *sc in lower back bar of next 15 sts, sk next st, sc in lower back bar of next 15 sts; rep from * around, join in first sc. (240 sts)

Rnd 27: Change to 6mm hook, ch 1, hdc in each st around, join in first hdc. Note: It's easy to inadvertently increase an extra hdc at the joining of rounds; count sts every few rows to ensure you aren't increasing.

Continue with green until there isn't enough yarn on the ball to finish a whole rnd. End with 2nd to last st of rnd. Yo, insert hook in last st, with black, yo, and pull through 3 lps on hook, join in first hdc (color change complete).

Rep rnd 27 with black until there isn't enough yarn on the ball to finish a whole rnd. Change to green the same way.

Alternate between green and black balls of yarn until the side measures approximately 13 ¾ inches (35cm), changing to green in last st if currently in a black stripe.

Last rnd: Ch 1, sc in each st around, join in first sc. Fasten off. Weave in ends.

LID

Rnd 1: With 6.5mm hook and green, form adjustable ring and make 7 sc in ring, join in first sc. (7 sc)

Rnd 2: Ch 1, 2hdc in each st around, join in first hdc. (14 hdc)

Rnd 3: Ch 1, [1 hdc, 2hdc in each of next 2 sts] 4 times, 2hdc in each of next 2 sts, join in first hdc. (24 hdc)

Rnd 4: Ch 1, hdc in same st as join, *1 hdc, 2hdc in next st, place sm in 2nd st just made**, 1 hdc; rep from * around, ending final rep at **, join in first hdc. (32 hdc)

Rnd 5: Ch 1, hdc in same st as join, *hdc across to st before marked st, 2hdc in next st, move sm to 2nd st just made; rep from * around, ending with hdc across to end, join in first hdc. (40 hdc)

Rnd 6: Ch 1, hdc in same st as join, *hdc across to marked st, 2hdc in marked st, move sm to first of 2 hdc just made, 1 hdc, 2hdc in next st; rep from * around, ending with hdc across to end, join in first hdc. (56 hdc)

Rnd 7: Ch 1, hdc in same st as join, *hdc across to st before marked st, 2hdc in next st, move sm to 2nd st just made; rep from * around, ending with hdc across to end, join in first hdc. (64 hdc)

Rnd 8: Ch 1, hdc in same st as join, *hdc across to and into marked st, 2hdc in next st, move sm to 2nd st just made; rep from * around, ending with hdc across to end, join in first hdc. (72 hdc)

Rnd 9: Ch 1, hdc in same st as join, *hdc across to marked st, 2hdc in marked st, move sm to first of 2 hdc just made, 3 hdc, 2hdc in next st; rep from * around, ending with hdc across to end, join in first hdc. (88 hdc)

Rnds 10–24: Rep rnds 7–9. (248 sts)

Rnd 25: Ch 1, hdc in each st around. (248 sts)

Rnd 26: Rep row 26 as for Sides. Fasten off.

FACIAL FEATURES

Create faces using the Facial Features instructions starting on page 16. Mix and match as desired. If you wish to create the face shown in the photographed project, consult the grid on page 34. Referring to the photographs or according to your own preferences, with sewing thread and needle, attach facial features to Lid of project. For mouth and eyebrows, sew on both sides of crocheted pieces to attach firmly.

ASSEMBLY

Weave in all ends.

LINING

Out of fabric, cut (2) 15 x 39-inch (38cm x 1m) rectangles and (2) 25-inch (63cm)-diameter circles. Sew two short ends of rectangles together with ¹/₂-inch (13mm) seam allowance to form a 15 x 77-inch (38cm x 2m)-long rectangle. Sew one long side of rectangle to outside edge of a circle with ¹/₂-inch (13mm) seam allowance. When the circle edge seam is complete, sew the other two short edges of the rectangle together with ¹/₂-inch (13mm) seam allowance.

Sew a ¹/₄-inch (6mm) rolled hem around the other circle and baste to the WS of the Lid. Baste the fabric "bowl" to the inside of the crocheted ottoman. Fill with foam peanuts or other beanbag-type filler. With yarn and tapestry needle, sew Lid to bottom of ottoman with mattress stitch (see page 14).

CHILLIN' OUT CUSHION

These cool colors remind me of swimming in an unused quarry that was filled with rain water. It was a perfect place for teenagers to go hang out and cool off on a summer day. The emoji has a ton of attitude, too. Make this pillow for someone with a "man cave" or a personal retreat where they like to relax and chill.

FINISHED MEASUREMENTS
14¼ inches (36cm) square

GAUGE
14 sts = 4 inches (10cm)
10 rows = 4 inches (10cm)

MEDIUM

MATERIALS + TOOLS

- Medium/worsted weight yarn (100% acrylic), 6 oz (170g) / 315 yds (288m) per ball, in the following colors:
  - 1 ball, cool green
  - 1 ball, green
  - 1 ball, black
  - 1 ball, teal
- 1 14-in. (35cm) square pillow form
- Matching sewing thread
- Sewing needle
- 1 14-in. (35cm) plastic zipper
- Sharp tapestry needle
- 5.5mm hook or size needed to achieve gauge

SPECIAL STITCHES

Foundation half-double crochet (fhdc): Ch 2, yo, insert hook in first ch, yo, pull through, yo, pull through first lp on hook (foundation ch made), yo, pull through 3 lps on hook (first fhdc made), *insert hook in lower 2 strands of foundation ch, yo, pull through, yo, pull through first lp on hook, yo, pull through 3 lps on hook; rep from * indicated number of times.

FACIAL FEATURES DIRECTORY

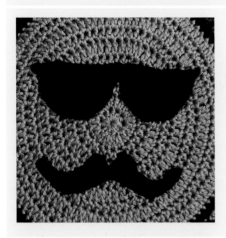

Use the facial elements from Crocheted Facial Features (page 16) to customize your emoji design. Just be sure to use yarn that is the same weight as the rest of your project to keep the face proportional.

Eyes: Sunglasses, First Lens; Sunglasses, 2nd Lens and Frames

Other: Moustache

FACIAL FEATURES

With green, work rnds 1–10 of Yellow Face from page 30. Fasten off.

Last rnd: Join black in any st, sc in same st as join, [2sc in next st, 16 sc] 6 times, sc in each rem st around, join in first st. Fasten off and weave in ends.

Create faces using the Facial Features instructions starting on page 16. Mix and match as desired. If you wish to create the faces shown in the photographed project, consult the grid at left. Referring to the photographs or according to your own preferences, with sewing thread and needle, attach facial features to project.

Sew face centered onto side of cushion that doesn't have the join seam.

PILLOW COVER

Row 1 (WS): With cool green, make 60 fhdc (see Special Stitches), turn.

Now working in rnds:

Rnd 1: Ch 1, hdc around, join in first hdc (being careful not to twist the foundation strip); gap will be sewn closed with yarn tail during finishing.

Rnd 2: Ch 1, hdc in same st as join, hdc in lower back bar on far side of next hdc, (hdc in next st, hdc in lower back bar of next hdc) around, sk the st that made the prev join, join in first hdc.

Rnds 3–5: Rep rnd 2.

Rnd 6: Rep rnd 2 to last st, yo, insert hook in lower back bar of next hdc, yo, pull through, with black, yo, pull through 3 lps on hook, join in first hdc.

Rnd 7: Rep rnd 6, but change to green.

Rnd 8: Rep rnd 6, but change to black.

Rnd 9: Rep rnd 6, but change to teal.

Rnds 10–13: Rep rnd 2.

Rnds 14–16: Rep rnds 6–8.

Rnds 17: Rep rnd 6, but change to cool green.

Rnds 18–33: Rep rnds 3–17.

Rnds 34–39: Rep rnd 2. Do not fasten off.

FINISHING

Working through both layers across top, work sc across by *inserting hook in lower back bar of front layer of cover and then through flo of corresponding st on back layer, yo, pull up lp, yo, pull through both lps on hook; rep from * across. Fasten off.

Weave in ends, closing gap at foundation ch.

Insert zipper in lower opening.

SWEET STUFF CUSHION

Although my boys had dolls to play with when they were little and no art project was considered off-limits or not-for-boys, they strongly disliked the pink and purple aisle in the toy section of department stores. So this was my first chance to design something pink and pretty! This emoji was the perfect fit for this throw cushion, which I can picture in a princess's room.

FINISHED MEASUREMENTS
14¼ inches (36cm) square

GAUGE
In pattern, 14 sts = 4 inches (10cm), 7 rows = 3 inches (7.5cm). Check gauge to save time.

MATERIALS + TOOLS

- DK weight yarn (100% acrylic), 5 oz (140g) / 362 yds (331m) per ball, in the following colors:
  - 1 ball, pink
  - 1 ball, red
  - 1 ball, blue
- 1 14-in. (35cm)-square pillow form
- Fading ink fabric marker
- Matching sewing thread
- Sewing needle
- 3¾-in. (10cm) buttons to match, or 14-in. (35cm) plastic zipper
- Locking stitch markers
- Sharp tapestry needle
- 5mm hook or size needed to achieve gauge

SPECIAL STITCHES

Herringbone half-double crochet (hhdc): Yo, insert hook in indicated st or sp, yo, pull lp through fabric and through first lp on hook, yo, pull through 2 lps on hook.

Linked double crochet (ldc): Insert hook under middle horizontal strand of prev dc, yo, pull lp through, insert hook in next st, yo, pull lp through, [yo, pull through 2 lps on hook] twice. To start a ldc row, ch 2 (does not count as st), insert hook in blo of 2nd ch from hook and pull up lp, insert hook into first st at base of ch-2, yo, pull lp through, finish dc as usual.

Decrease (dec): Yo, insert hook in next st, yo, pull lp through, insert hook in next st, yo, pull through all lps on hook.

Surface slip stitch (sslst): Insert hook through fabric in a spot on drawn line, yo, pull up lp, *insert hook in next spot along drawn line, yo, pull lp through fabric and lp on hook; rep from * around drawn line.

FACIAL FEATURES DIRECTORY

Use the facial elements from Crocheted Facial Features (page 16) to customize your emoji design. Just be sure to use yarn that is the same weight as the rest of your project to keep the face proportional.

Eyes: Hearts, Medium
Mouth: Mouth, Extra-Large
Other: Eyebrows

CENTER SQUARE

Make 2.

Row 1: With pink, ch 45, hdc in back ridge of 2nd ch from hook, hdc in back ridge of each ch across, turn. (44 sts)

Row 2–3: Ch 1, hhdc (see Special Stitches) in each st across, turn.

Row 4: Ch 2, ldc (see Special Stitches) in each st across, turn.

Rows 5–28: Rep rows 2–4.

Rows 29–30: Rep rows 2–3.

Row 31: Ch 1, hdc in each st across. Fasten off.

FIRST SQUARE EDGING

Make 2 if using a zipper to close pillow cover.

Fold Center Square in half along rows and mark with sm at halfway point on one side.

Rnd 1: With red, join yarn with sl st in marked side, 21 sc evenly along side working in ends of rows to corner, 3sc in corner st, 42 sc evenly along top of sts, 3sc in corner st, 42 sc evenly along side in ends of rows, 3sc in next corner, 42 sc evenly along top of sts, 3sc in corner, 21 sc evenly along side in ends of rows, join in first sc. (180 sts)

Rnd 2: Ch 1, hhdc in same st as join, [hhdc in each st across to middle of 3 corner sts, (hhdc, sc, hhdc) in corner st] 4 times, hhdc across to beg of rnd being careful not to work into sl st from prev rnd, join in first hhdc. (188 sts)

Rnd 3: Ch 1, hdc in same st as join, [hdc in each st to corner-sc, 2hdc in corner-sc] 4 times, hdc across to beg of rnd. Finish with sewn invisible join (see page 13).

EDGING WITH BUTTONHOLE FLAP

Wind a 1 oz (25g) ball of red yarn.

With main ball of yarn, rep rnds 1–2 from First Square Edging, remove lp from hook and place on locking sm.

Row 3: With WS facing, in any corner sc, join 2nd ball of yarn, sc in same st as join, hdc in next st, place sm in st just made, hhdc across to 1 st before corner st, dec (see Special Stitches) in next 2 sts, turn. (43 sts)

Row 4: Ch 1, sk first st, sc in next st, hdc in next st, place sm in st just made, hhdc in each st across to 1 st before marked st, dec in next 2 sts, turn. (41 sts)

Rows 5–6: Rep row 4. (37 sts)

Row 7: Ch 1, sk first st, sc in next st, hdc in next st, move sm to st just made, 5 hhdc, [ch 2, sk 2 sts, 10 hhdc] twice,

ch 2, sk 2 sts, hhdc in each st across to 1 st before marked st, dec in next 2 sts, turn. (29 sts, 3 ch-2 sps)

Row 8: Rep row 4, working into chs, not the sps of the buttonholes. (33 sts)

Row 9: Rep row 4. (31 sts) Fasten off.

Return lp on locking st market to hook, ch 1, hdc in same st as join, hdc in each st around, working 2hdc in each of 4 corners, and working 7 hdc evenly across each diagonal side of buttonband, join in first st. Fasten off. Weave in all ends.

FACIAL FEATURES

Center a 9 to 10-inch (23 to 25cm) diameter bowl or other circular object on the Square with Buttonhole Flap (or either square if closing with zipper) and trace around it with a fading ink fabric marker. With blue, work sslst (see Special Stitches) around.

Create faces using the Facial Features instructions starting on page 16. Mix and match as desired. If you wish to create the faces shown in the photographed project, consult the grid above. Referring to the photographs or according to your own preferences, with sewing thread and needle, attach facial features to project.

ASSEMBLY

With RS held tog, and with yarn, whip stitch through the lower back bar of the hdc's around 3 edges. Turn RS out. Sew 3 buttons on plain square to correspond to holes or insert zipper in opening.

TAUNTING MEGA CUSHION

Big throw cushions are a dream to lean against and to prop yourself up while crocheting or relaxing. Puff stitches look great in rows, but I really like arranging them in hexagonal format because they look fun to touch and there are so many paths to trace on them with your fingers, like a big Chinese checkers game board. Try any of the faces provided in these charts, or use the template on page 49 to design your own.

FINISHED MEASUREMENTS
30 inches (76cm) square

GAUGE
In bobble stitch pattern:
12 bobbles = 9 inches (23cm)
7 bobble rows (14 pattern rows) = 4 1/2 inches (11cm)

In dc:
13 dc = 4 inches (10cm);
7 dc rows = 4 inches (10cm)

MEDIUM

MATERIALS + TOOLS

- Worsted weight yarn (100% acrylic), 3.5 oz (100g) / 200yds (180m) per ball, in the following colors:
  - 3 balls, purple
  - 1 ball, black
  - 2 balls, light yellow
  - 2 balls, light green
  - 2 balls, teal
  - 1 ball, red
- 6mm hook or size needed to achieve gauge

SPECIAL STITCHES

Bobble: [Yo, insert hook in indicated st, yo, draw up lp, yo, draw through first 2 lps on hook] 4 times in same st, yo, draw through 5 lps on hook.

PREPARATION

Wind small amounts (25 g) of the following colors onto bobbins, clothespins, or into hand-wound balls with hair clips to stop them from unravelling: 1 ball purple, 2 balls yellow, 4 balls black, 1 ball red, 1 ball green, 1 ball teal.

BOBBLE STITCH PATTERN

Note: Bobbles (see Special Stitches) are worked across WS rows as they push out to the RS.

Make 24 fsc sts.

Row 1: Ch 1, sc in each st across, turn.

Row 2 (WS): Ch 1, sc in first 2 sts, [bobble in next st, sc in next st] across, turn.

Row 3 (RS): Ch 1, sc in each st across, turn.

Row 4: Ch 1, sc in first st, [bobble in next st, sc in next st] across to last st, sc in last st, turn.

Rep rows 1–4 for swatch.

Note that every other row, the extra sc moves from one side of the work to the other side so that the bobbles shift over by one st every other row.

FOLLOWING THE CHART

On the charts shown starting on page 46, each row of hexagons consists of both RS and WS rows. Right-handed crocheters read across from right to left every RS row and from left to right every WS row for the same row of hexagons. The indentations at either side of the hexagon rows indicate where the extra sc is worked.

CHANGING COLORS

Every color block on the chart consists of 2 sc side by side on a RS row; on the WS row, the bobble is worked into the first sc in the same color and a sc is worked into the 2nd sc of the same color.

When you work across the RS row, you work to the point where you need to change colors. The last sc in the old color is worked as follows: Insert hook into next st, yo, pull up lp. Then you place a strand of the new color across the hook and pull it through the 2 lps on the hook, then work a sc into each of the next 2 sts.

When you work across the WS row (for the same row of hexagons in the chart), you work a bobble and then a sc for the same hexagon. To change to a new color, work to the last st in the old color, then in that last st, insert hook and draw up a lp with the old color; then with the new color, yo and pull through the sc, and the next bobble is done in the new color, too. At all times the unused colors of yarn should be loosely stranded across the WS of the fabric.

CUSHION COVER, FRONT

With purple, work 76 fsc sts.

[Work rows 1–4 of Bobble Stitch Pattern] twice.

ROW 5 OF CHART

RS: Ch 1, 26 sc. Work next sc and change to black in last yo and pull through, work 24 sc in black, changing to purple in 24th sc, 26 sc, turn.

WS: Ch 1, 2 sc, [bobble, sc] 12 times, changing to black in last yo and pull through, [bobble, sc] 12 times, changing to purple in last yo and pull through, [bobble, sc] 13 times.

ROW 6 OF CHART

RS: Ch 1, 23 sc, change to black in last yo and pull through, in black, 30 sc, changing to purple in last yo, pull through, with purple, 23 sc, turn.

WS: Ch 1, sc in first st, [bobble, sc] 11 times, change to black in last yo and pull through, in black, [bobble, sc] 15 times, change to purple in last yo and pull through, in purple [bobble, sc] 11 times, sc in last st, turn.

ROW 7 OF CHART

RS: Ch 1, 20 sc, change to black in last yo and pull through, 6 sc, change to yellow in last yo and pull through, 24 sc in yellow, change to black in last pull through, 6 sc, change to purple in last yo and pull through, sc in rem sts, turn.

WS: Ch 1, 2 sc, [bobble, sc] 9 times, change to black, [bobble, sc] 3 times, change to yellow, [bobble sc] 12 times, change to black, [bobble, sc] 3 times, change to purple, [bobble, sc] 10 times, turn.

ROW 8 OF CHART

RS: Ch 1, 17 sc, change to black, 6 sc, change to light yellow, 30 sc, change to black, 6 sc, change to purple, 17 sc.

WS: Ch 1, sc in first st, [bobble, sc] 8 times, change to black, [bobble, sc] 3 times, change to light yellow, [bobble, sc] 15 times, change to black, [bobble, sc] 3 times, change to purple, [bobble, sc] 8 times, sc in last st, turn.

ROWS 9–85 OF CHART

Follow chart as established.

ROW 86 OF CHART

Ch 1, sc in each st across. Fasten off.

CUSHION COVER, BACK

Row 1: With purple, ch 100, dc in 4th ch from hook and in each ch across, turn. (98 dc)

Rows 2–15: Ch 3, dc across, turn.

Row 16: Ch 3, dc across to last st, with purple, yo, insert hook, yo, pull up lp, yo, pull through first 2 lps on hook, with light green (leaving a 5-inch [13cm] tail), yo, pull through last 2 lps on hook, turn.

Row 17: With green, ch 3, lay purple across tops of next 5 sts, with light green dc in next 5 sts trapping purple underneath, yo, insert hook in next st, yo, pull up lp, yo, pull through first 2 lps on hook, with purple, yo, pull through last 2 lps on hook, bring light green yarn to front between hook and purple yarn, lay light green across tops of next 6 sts, with purple, dc across next 6 sts trapping light green underneath, dc across rem sts.

Row 18: Ch 3, dc in each st across to light green yarn, with purple, yo, insert hook in next st, yo, pull up lp, yo, pull through first 2 lps on hook, with light green, yo, pull through last 2 lps on hook, bring purple yarn to front between hook and light green yarn**, with light green, dc rem sts across, turn.

Row 19: Ch 3, dc in each st across to purple yarn, *lay purple across tops of next 5 sts, with green dc in next 5 sts trapping purple underneath, yo, insert hook in next st, yo, pull up lp, yo, pull through first 2 lps on hook, with purple, yo, pull through last 2 lps on hook, bring light green yarn to front between hook and purple yarn, lay light green

across tops of next 6 sts, with purple, dc across next 6 sts trapping light green underneath, dc across rem sts, turn.

Rows 20–27: [Rep rows 16 and 17] 4 times.

Row 28: Rep row 16 to last st, yo, insert hook in last st, yo, pull up lp, yo, pull through first 2 lps on hook, with teal (leaving a 5-inch [13cm] tail), yo, pull through last 2 lps, turn.

Row 29: With teal, ch 3, lay green across tops of next 5 sts, with teal dc in next 5 sts trapping light green underneath, yo, insert hook in next st, yo, pull up lp, yo, pull through first 2 lps on hook, with light green, yo, pull through last 2 lps on hook, bring teal yarn to front between hook and light green yarn, lay teal across tops of next 6 sts, with light green, dc across next 6 sts trapping teal

underneath, dc across to purple yarn, work row 19 from * to end.

Row 30: Rep row 18 to **, with light green, dc across to teal yarn, with light green, yo, insert hook in next st, yo, pull up lp, yo, pull through first 2 lps on hook, with teal, yo, pull through last 2 lps on hook, bring light green yarn to front between hook and teal yarn, with teal dc rem sts across, turn.

Next 22 rows: Continue as established, changing colors every 6 sts until there are no more purple stitches, and then until there are no more light green stitches, then work only in teal. Cut yarn of colors no longer in use when necessary. (52 rows total)

Weave in ends.

Taunting Pattern

Pattern is not to scale. Refer to instructions on Following the
Chart on page 44. Colors shown correspond to yarn colors.

Love Pattern

Pattern is not to scale. Colors shown correspond to yarn colors.

Smile Pattern

Pattern is not to scale. Colors shown correspond to yarn colors.

Template

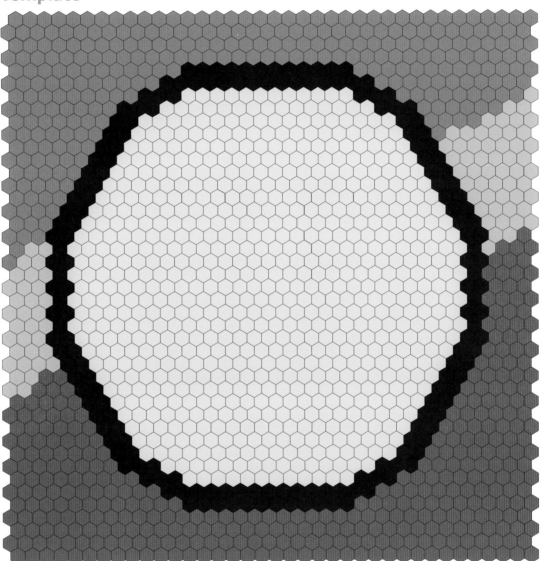

Pattern is not to scale. Colors shown correspond to yarn colors.
Photocopy this template and fill in an emoji design of your choice.

9 FACES LAPGHAN

The squares in this blanket bring fun, texture, and cheer to any home. These 9 squares make a great lapghan, but simply add more squares to crochet a larger piece and add the emojis of your choice that will keep you cheery as you snuggle under it during screen time or to chase away the chill of a grey day. There are 18 emoji options for this blanket. You can choose the 9 shown, or mix in some of the others!

FINISHED MEASUREMENTS
Each block with border =
11½ inches (29cm) square
Finished blanket with border =
35 inches (89cm) square

GAUGE
14 sc and 14.5 sc rows =
4 inches (10cm)
Exact gauge isn't essential
for this project

MATERIALS + TOOLS

- Worsted weight yarn (100% acrylic), 6 oz (170 g) / 315 yds (288m) per ball, in the following colors:
  - 1 ball, yellow
  - 2 balls, plum
  - 1 ball, peach
  - 1 ball, light pink
  - 2 balls, medium purple
  - 1 ball, medium pink
  - 2 balls, light purple
  - 1 ball, light blue
- 5.5mm hook or size needed to achieve gauge

SPECIAL STITCHES

Bobble: The bobble stitch is worked over 2 sts; in the first st work (insert hook, pull up lp, yo, pull through first lp on hook (2 lps on hook), yo, insert hook in same st, pull up lp, yo, pull through first lp on hook, yo, pull through 2 lps on hook (3 lps on hook), insert hook in same st and pull up lp (4 lps on hook), yo, pull through all 4 lps, sc in 2nd st.

PATTERN NOTES

- Bobbles (see Special Stitches) are worked in a different color than the background color of each square. Plum is used for all dark squares in chart. Light blue and light pink are used for colored accents such as rosy cheeks, hearts, tears, or the halo.

- Wrap the small amounts (.7 to .9 oz [20 to 25g]) of yarn for emoji faces on bobbins.

- When starting a row, all strands of yarn and bobbins should be at the back of the piece away from the crocheter; when ending a row, all strands of yarn and bobbins should be at the side of the piece facing the crocheter.

- Color changes happen in the last st of the old color and the next st in the new color as follows: With old color, insert hook in next st and pull up lp; with new color, yo and pull through, bring old color yarn from back of work to front of work between the hook and the strand of new color and hold to the side; work bobble or sc in new color in next st as indicated.

- Charts are read from left to right for WS rows and right to left for RS rows. Each block on chart represents 4 sts: 2 on WS row and 2 on RS row.

- When bobbles of the same color appear stacked above each other in the same column, a sc should be worked in each of the 2 bobble stitches when returning on the RS in the same color. If the next bobble above in any given column is not the same color, the 2 sc on the RS should be worked in the color of the 2 sts above (represented by a T block in the chart).

SQUARES: SMILEY EMOJI

The text instructions for this block are provided here. As you follow the text pattern, follow the large chart (see pg 54) as well, so that you get used to reading the chart; the other faces will only be in chart form. You will need 9 charts total.

Row 1 (WS): With yellow, ch 41, sc in 2nd ch from hook and in each ch across, turn. (40 sc)

Row 2: Ch 1, sc across, turn.

Row 3: Ch 1, 14 sc, changing to plum in last sc (see Pattern Notes), [bobble, sc] 6 times, changing to yellow with an additional bobbin in last sc, 14 sc, turn.

Row 4: Ch 1, 26 sc in yellow, change to first bobbin with yellow yarn (there is a bobbin with yellow for either side of the mouth), 14 sc, turn.

Row 5: Ch 1, 10 sc in yellow, change to new plum bobbin, [bobble, sc] twice, change to yellow, 12 sc, change to plum yarn and working over strand of yellow yarn (see Pattern Notes), [bobble, sc] twice, change to yellow, 10 sc, turn.

Row 6: Ch 1, 30 sc in yellow, trapping plum yarn across, change to other strand of yellow, sc across rem sts.

Row 7: Ch 1, 8 sc, change to plum, trapping extra strand from prev row, work bobble, sc, change to yellow, 20 sc, change to plum, trapping yellow yarn in next sts, work bobble, sc, change to yellow, 8 sc, turn.

Row 8: Ch 1, 30 sc in yellow, trapping plum yarn across, change to next strand of yellow and sc across rem sts.

Row 9: Ch 1, 6 sc, change to plum, trapping extra strand from prev row, work bobble, sc, change to yellow, 24 sc, change to plum, trapping yellow yarn in next sts, work bobble, sc, change to yellow, 6 sc, turn.

Row 10: Ch 1, 32 sc, trapping plum across, sc in next 2 sts, change to first yellow yarn, 6 sc, turn.

Row 11: Ch 1, 4 sc, change to plum, trapping extra strand from prev row, work bobble, sc, change to yellow, 8 sc, change to new plum bobbin, [bobble, sc] 6 times, change to new yellow bobbin, 8 sc, change to plum, trapping yellow yarn in next sts, work bobble, sc, change to yellow, 4 sc, turn.

Row 12: Ch 1, 4 sc, change to plum, trapping yellow yarn in next sts, work 2 sc, change to yellow, 20 sc, change to next yellow, 8 sc, change to plum, 2 sc, change to yellow, 4 sc, turn.

Row 13: Ch 1, 4 sc, change to plum, bobble, sc, change to yellow, 6 sc, join new plum bobbin, bobble, sc, change to yellow, 12 sc, change to plum, bobble, sc, change to yellow, 6 sc, change to plum, trapping yellow yarn in next sts, work bobble, sc, change to yellow, 4 sc, turn.

Row 14: Ch 1, 26 sc, trapping plum across, sc in next 2 sts, change to next yellow, 6 sc, trapping plum across, sc in next 2 sts, change to next yellow, 4 sc.

Row 15: Ch 1, 2 sc, change to plum, trapping extra strand from prev row, bobble, sc, change to yellow, 6 sc, change to plum, trapping extra strand from prev row, bobble, sc, change to yellow, 16 sc, change to plum, bobble, sc, change to yellow, 6 sc, change to plum 2 sc, change to yellow, 2 sc, turn.

Row 16: Ch 1, 2 sc, change to plum, 2 sc, change to yellow, 8 sc, 16 sc, trapping plum across, 2 sc, change to next yellow, 6 sc, change to plum, 2 sc, change to yellow, 2 sc, turn.

Row 17: Ch 1, 2 sc, change to plum, bobble, sc, change to yellow, 4 sc, change to plum, trapping extra strand from prev row, bobble, sc, change to yellow, 20 sc, change to Plum, bobble, sc, change to yellow, 4 sc, change to plum, 2 sc, change to yellow, 2 sc, turn.

Row 18: Ch 1, 2 sc, change to plum, 2 sc, change to yellow, 32 sc, change to plum, 2 sc, change to yellow, 2 sc, turn.

Row 19: Ch 1, 2 sc, change to plum, bobble, sc, change to yellow, 32 sc, change to plum, bobble, sc, change to yellow, 2 sc, turn.

Row 20: Ch 1, 2 sc, change to plum, 2 sc, change to yellow, 32 sc, change to plum, 2 sc, change to yellow, 2 sc, turn.

Rows 21–24: Rep rows 19–20.

Row 25: Ch 1, 2 sc, change to plum, bobble, sc, change to yellow, 8 sc, change to plum, [bobble, sc] 3 times, change to new yellow bobbin, 4 sc, change to new plum bobbin, [bobble, sc] 3 times, change to new yellow bobbin, 8 sc, change to plum, bobble, sc, change to yellow, 2 sc, turn.

Row 26: Ch 1, 2 sc, trapping plum across, sc in next 4 sts, 6 sc, change to plum, 6 sc, change to yellow, 4 sc, change to plum, 6 sc, change to yellow, change to last yellow, trapping other yarns where necessary, sc across rem sts, turn.

Row 27: Ch 1, 4 sc, change to plum, bobble, sc, change to yellow 6 sc, change to plum, [bobble, sc] 3 times, change to yellow, 4 sc, change to plum, [bobble, sc] 3 times, change to yellow, 6 sc, change to plum and trapping yarn across, bobble, sc, change to yellow 4 sc, turn.

Row 28: Ch 1, 4 sc, change to plum, 2 sc, change to yellow, 8 sc, change to plum 4 sc, change to yellow, 6 sc, change to plum 4 sc, change to yellow, 6 sc, change to plum, 2 sc, change to yellow, 4 sc, turn.

Row 29: Ch 1, 4 sc, change to plum, bobble, sc, change to yellow, 6 sc, change to plum, [bobble, sc] 2 times, change to yellow, 6 sc, change to plum, [bobble, sc] 2 times, change to yellow 8 sc, change to plum, bobble, sc, change to yellow, 4 sc, turn.

Row 30: Ch 1, 4 sc, trapping plum where necessary, and changing yellow strand, 36 sc across, turn.

Row 31: Ch 1, 6 sc, change to plum, bobble, sc, change to yellow, 24 sc, change to plum, bobble, sc, change to yellow, 6 sc, turn.

Row 32: Ch 1, trapping plum where necessary and changing from one yellow bobbin to the next where they meet, 40 sc across, turn.

Row 33: Ch 1, 8 sc, change to plum, bobble, sc, change to yellow, 20 sc, change to plum, bobble, sc, change to yellow, 8 sc, turn.

Row 34: Rep row 32.

Row 35: Ch 1, 10 sc, change to plum, [bobble, sc] twice, change to yellow, 12 sc, change to plum, [bobble, sc] twice, change to yellow, 10 sc, turn.

Row 36: Rep row 32.

Row 37: Ch 1, 14 sc, change to plum, [bobble, sc] 6 times, change to yellow, 14 sc, turn.

Row 38: Rep row 32.

Rows 39–40: Ch 1, 40 sc across, turn. Do not fasten off.

EDGING

Row 1: Rotate work 90 degrees to work across side, with same color as background (sc, ch 1, sc) in end of row, sc 38 evenly across side, (sc, ch 1, sc) in corner, 38 sc evenly across opposite side of starting ch, (sc, ch 1, sc) in corner, 38 sc evenly across next side, (sc, ch 1, sc) in next corner, 38 sc evenly across top, sl st in first st to join. (160 sc) Fasten off.

Row 2: With plum, start with hdc in any stitch, [hdc in each st across to next corner, 2 hdc in corner ch-sp] 4 times, hdc in each st across to beginning, sl st in first hdc. (48 hdc) Fasten off.

SQUARES: OTHER FACES

All background colors are worked in sc, any facial features and hearts are made in bobbles. The following colors and charts are as shown in the photographed project, but feel free to mix and match other faces from pages 54 to 61 to your heart's content. After crocheting the emoji faces, edge them as done for Squares: Smiley Emoji.

Winky: Peach background; plum for contrasting color; light pink for tongue.

Kissy: Medium purple background; plum for contrasting color; light pink for heart.

Infatuation: Medium pink background; plum for contrasting color; light pink for hearts.

Rosy Cheeks: Light purple background; plum for contrasting color; light pink for cheeks.

Angel: Light purple background; plum for contrasting color; blue for halo.

Feeling Blue: Blue background; plum for contrasting color.

Cool Dude: Medium purple background; plum for contrasting color.

D'oh!: Light pink background; plum for contrasting color.

ASSEMBLY

Top row from left to right: Winky, Kissy, Infatuation.

Middle row from left to right: Rosy Cheeks, Smiley, Angel.

Bottom row from left to right: Feeling Blue, Cool Dude, D'oh!

With RS of squares held together, whip stitch seam through extra hdc lp only across.

Weave in all ends.

FINAL EDGING

With blue, start with sc in any corner across, ch 2, sc in same corner, [159 sc evenly across side, (sc, ch 2, sc) in next corner] 3 times, 159 sc evenly across, sl st in first st to join. Fasten off.

With peach, start with sc in any corner ch-sp, ch 2, sc in same corner st, *[ch 1, sk next st, sc in next st] 60 times evenly across, ch 1**, (sc, ch 2, sc) in next corner ch-sp; rep from * across, ending final rep at **, sl st in first sc to join. Fasten off.

With medium pink, start with sc in any corner ch-sp, 1 sc in same corner sp, *[ch 1, sc in next ch-sp] across to next corner, ch 1**, 3sc in next corner sp; rep from * around, ending final rep at **, sc in first corner sp, sl st in first sc to join. Fasten off.

With plum, start with hdc in any st, hdc in each st and sp around working 2 hdc in each corner st, sl st to join in first hdc. Fasten off.

Smiley Pattern

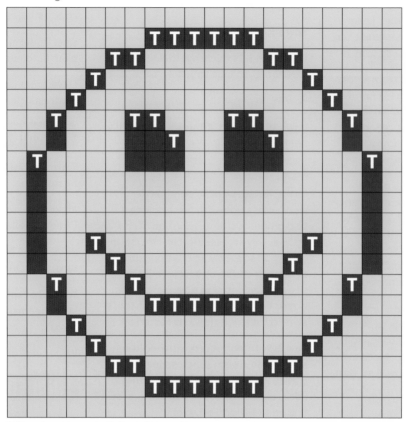

Pattern is not to scale. Refer to Pattern Notes on page 52.

Each block consists of 2 sts and 2 rows with the WS worked first and the RS row worked 2nd.

☐ = 2 sc on WS and 2 sc on RS

■ = Bobble, then sc on WS with contrasting color and 2 sc on RS in contrasting color

T = Bobble, then sc on WS with contrasting color and 2 sc on RS in color that will be used in these 2 sts in the next WS row

Winky Pattern

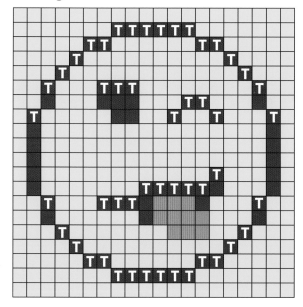

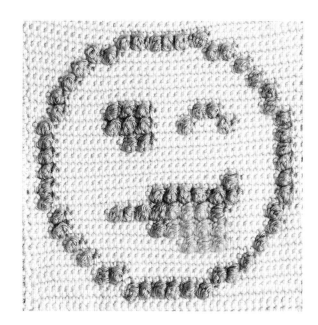

Kissy Pattern

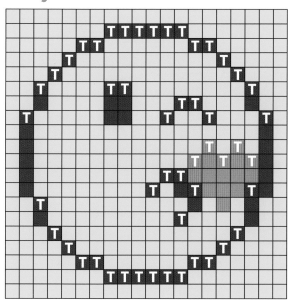

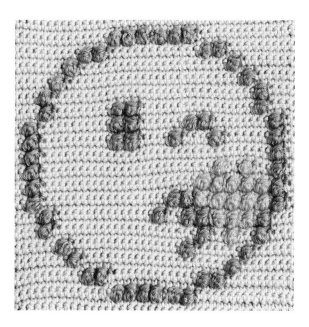

Each block consists of 2 sts and 2 rows with the WS worked first and the RS row worked 2nd.

☐ = 2 sc on WS and 2 sc on RS

■ = Bobble, then sc on WS with contrasting color and 2 sc on RS in contrasting color

T = Bobble, then sc on WS with contrasting color and 2 sc on RS in color that will be used in these 2 sts in the next WS row

▦ = Bobble, then sc, on WS with pink or red and 2 sc on RS in contrasting color

T = Bobble, then sc, on WS with pink or red and 2 sc on RS in pink or red

Infatuation Pattern

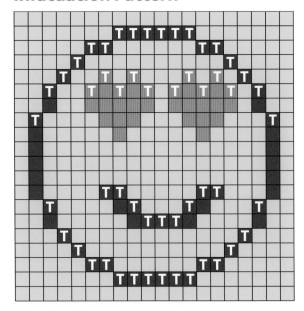
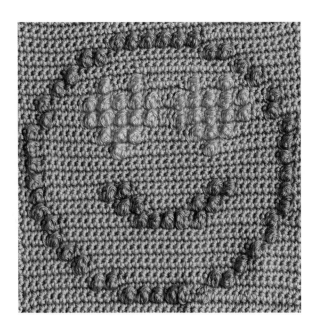

Rosy Cheeks Pattern

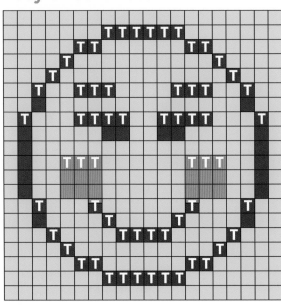
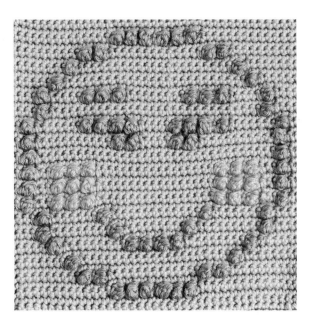

Each block consists of 2 sts and 2 rows with the WS worked first and the RS row worked 2nd.

= 2 sc on WS and 2 sc on RS

= Bobble, then sc on WS with contrasting color and 2 sc on RS in contrasting color

T = Bobble, then sc on WS with contrasting color and 2 sc on RS in color that will be used in these 2 sts in the next WS row

= Bobble, then sc, on WS with pink or red and 2 sc on RS in contrasting color

T = Bobble, then sc, on WS with pink or red and 2 sc on RS in pink or red

Angel Pattern

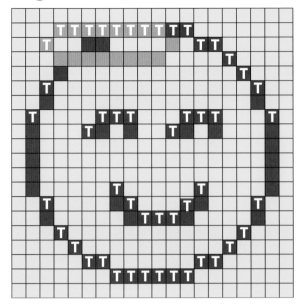

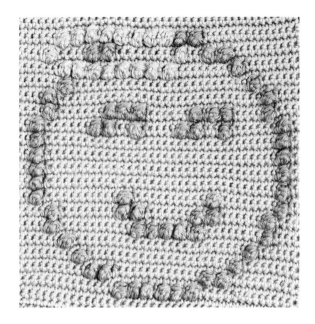

Feeling Blue Pattern

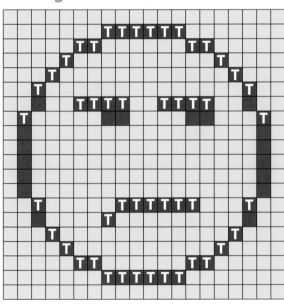

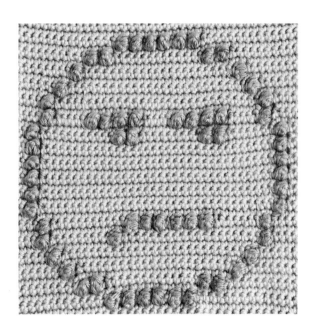

Each block consists of 2 sts and 2 rows with the WS worked first and the RS row worked 2nd.

= 2 sc on WS and 2 sc on RS

= Bobble, then sc on WS with contrasting color and 2 sc on RS in contrasting color

T = Bobble, then sc on WS with contrasting color and 2 sc on RS in color that will be used in these 2 sts in the next WS row

= Bobble, then sc, on WS with blue and 2 sc on RS in contrasting color

T = Bobble, then sc, on WS with blue and 2 sc on RS in blue

Cool Dude Pattern

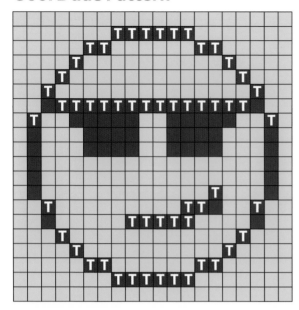

D'oh! Pattern

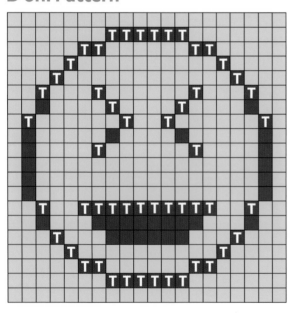

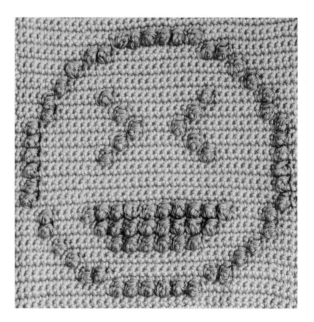

Each block consists of 2 sts and 2 rows with the WS worked first and the RS row worked 2nd.

☐ = 2 sc on WS and 2 sc on RS

■ = Bobble, then sc on WS with contrasting color and 2 sc on RS in contrasting color

T = Bobble, then sc on WS with contrasting color and 2 sc on RS in color that will be used in these 2 sts in the next WS row

Chillin' Pattern

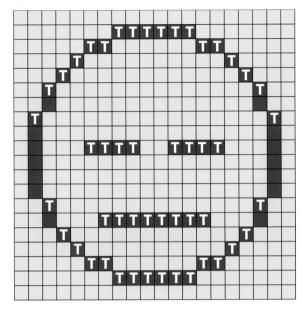

Blank Pattern

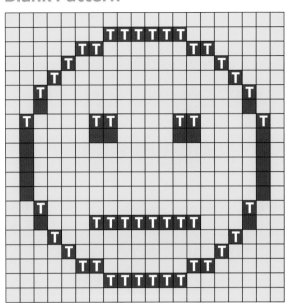

Determined Pattern

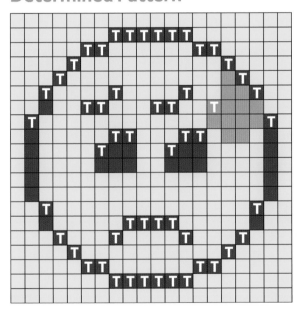

Each block consists of 2 sts and 2 rows with the WS worked first and the RS row worked 2nd.

☐ = 2 sc on WS and 2 sc on RS

■ = Bobble, then sc on WS with contrasting color and 2 sc on RS in contrasting color

T = Bobble, then sc on WS with contrasting color and 2 sc on RS in color that will be used in these 2 sts in the next WS row

▨ = Bobble, then sc, on WS with blue and 2 sc on RS in contrasting color

T = Bobble, then sc, on WS with blue and 2 sc on RS in blue

Grossed Out Pattern

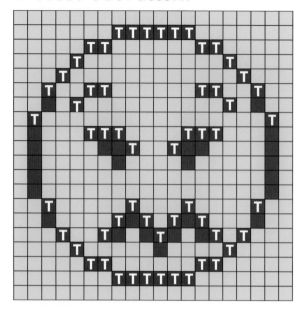

Thoughtful Pattern

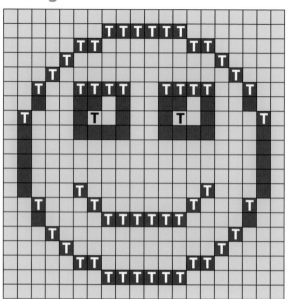

Grouchy Pattern

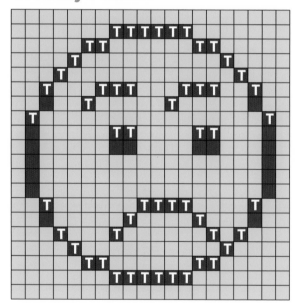

Each block consists of 2 sts and 2 rows with the WS worked first and the RS row worked 2nd.

☐ = 2 sc on WS and 2 sc on RS

T = Bobble, then sc on WS with yellow and 2 sc on RS in contasting color that will be used in these 2 sts in the next WS row

■ = Bobble, then sc on WS with contrasting color and 2 sc on RS in contrasting color

T = Bobble, then sc on WS with contrasting color and 2 sc on RS in color that will be used in these 2 sts in the next WS row

Surprise Pattern

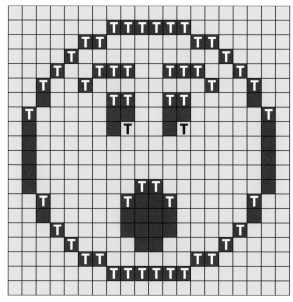

Schemer Pattern

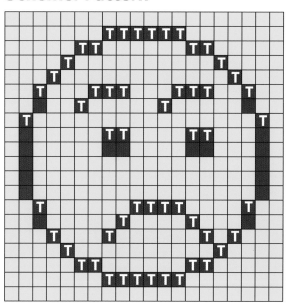

Anxious Pattern

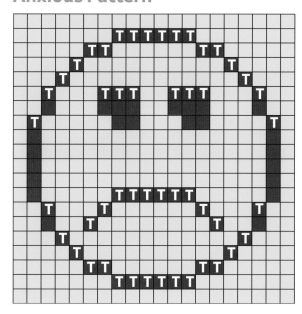

Each block consists of 2 sts and 2 rows with the WS worked first and the RS row worked 2nd.

= 2 sc on WS and 2 sc on RS

T = Bobble, then sc on WS with yellow and 2 sc on RS in contrasting color that will be used in these 2 sts in the next WS row

= Bobble, then sc on WS with contrasting color and 2 sc on RS in contrasting color

T = Bobble, then sc on WS with contrasting color and 2 sc on RS in color that will be used in these 2 sts in the next WS row

CLOTHES

From head to toe, this chapter's clothing will have you covered in emojis. Have a baby shower coming up? Try the Baby Beanies (page 64) and Num Num Bib (page 67) as a gift set. When it gets cold outside, bundle up with a Surly Slouchie Hat (page 73) or Pom-Pom Beanie (page 76), Kissy Pocket Scarf (page 80), and Not Too Blue for You Mittens (page 83). Keep toasty warm inside with Smelly Slippers (page 87) on your feet and a Big Grin Hoodie (page 90). No matter what clothing you choose to crochet, customize your look by choosing the emoji faces you prefer.

BABY BEANIES

These two little hats come with a lot of options. You can wear them with either side of the fabric facing out for a different look, and there are two brim versions you can choose from. Then, add emoji facial elements from page 16 to make your little ones look unique. This is a great opportunity to make faces with your favorite colors—not all emojis have to be yellow!

FINISHED MEASUREMENTS
Circumference: 17 inches (43cm)
Brim: 16 inches (41cm)

GAUGE
Worked in the round, 13 hdc = 4 inches (10cm); 11 hdc rnds = 4 inches (10cm)
First 6 rnds of hat = 2 ¼ inches (6cm) in diameter

LIGHT

MATERIALS + TOOLS

- DK weight yarn (70% acrylic, 30% merino wool), 3.5 oz (100g) / 260 yds (238m) per ball, in the following colors:
    - 1 ball, blue
    - 1 ball, black
    - A few yards, white
    - 1 ball, pink
- 5.5mm hook or size needed to achieve gauge
- 3.75mm hook or size needed to achieve gauge
- Locking stitch markers
- Less than 1 oz (28g) polyester fiber fill
- Matching sewing thread and needle
- Sharp tapestry needle

SPECIAL STITCHES

Split single crochet (split sc): When inserting hook, rather than going below usual 2 top strands, go between the 2 vertical legs of the next sc through to the other side of the fabric, yo, pull up lp to height of current rnd, yo, pull through 2 lps on hook.

Note: Join with sl st unless otherwise indicated.

FACIAL FEATURES DIRECTORY

Use the facial elements from Crocheted Facial Features (page 16) to customize your emoji design. Just be sure to use yarn that is the same weight as the rest of your project to keep the face proportional.

Eyes: Oval Eye, Medium
Mouth: Oval Eye, Large
Other: Eyebrows

Eyes: Round Eye with Pupil
Mouth: Mouth, Large

Rnd 22: Ch 1, [split sc (see Special Stitches) in next sc, fpdc around next dc] 28 times, join in first sc.

Rnds 23–25: Rep rnd 22. Fasten off.

FACIAL FEATURES

Create faces using the Facial Features instructions starting on page 16. Mix and match as desired. If you wish to create the faces shown in the photographed project, consult the grid at left. Referring to the photographs or according to your own preferences, with sewing thread and needle, attach facial features to project.

FINISHING

Weave in ends. Turn hat inside out. Flip brim up if desired and tack in place.

OH SO CUTE! PINK BEANIE

CROWN

With pink, work as for Blue Brilliance Beanie up to brim.

BRIM

Rnd 21: Turn hat inside out to work in opposite direction. Ch 1, [sc in next st, dc in lower back bar of next st (visible on WS of st)] 28 times, join in first sc.

Rnd 22: Ch 1, [split sc (see Special Stitches) in next sc, fpdc around next dc] 28 times, join in first sc.

Rnds 23–25: Rep rnd 22. Fasten off.

FACIAL FEATURES

Create faces using the Facial Features instructions starting on page 16. Mix and match as desired. If you wish to create the faces shown in the photographed project, consult the grid above. Referring to the photographs or according to your own preferences, with sewing thread and needle, attach facial features to project.

FINISHING

Weave in ends. Turn hat inside out. Flip brim up if desired and tack in place.

BLUE BRILLIANCE BEANIE

CROWN

Rnd 1: With blue, work 7 hdc into adjustable ring, join in first hdc. (7 hdc)

Rnd 2: Ch 1, 2hdc in each st around, join in first hdc. (14 hdc)

Rnd 3: Ch 1, [2hdc in next st, hdc in next st] 7 times, join in first hdc. (21 sts)

Rnd 4: Ch 1, [2 hdc, 2hdc in next st] 7 times, join in first hdc. (28 sts)

Rnd 5: Ch 1, [2hdc in next st, 2 hdc] 9 times, hdc in next st, join in first hdc. (37 sts)

Rnd 6: Ch 1, [3 hdc, 2hdc in next st] 9 times, hdc in next st, join in first hdc. (46 sts)

Rnd 7: Ch 1, 2 hdc, [2hdc in next st, 5 hdc] 7 times, 2 hdc, join in first hdc. (53 sts)

Rnd 8: Ch 1, 1 hdc, [8 hdc, 2hdc in next st, 8 hdc] 3 times, 1 hdc, join in first hdc. (56 sts)

SIDE

Rnds 9–20: Ch 1, hdc in each st around, ensuring to work last hdc in top of sl st of prev rnd and counting every rnd to maintain 56 sts per rnd, join in first hdc.

Work more rows for a deeper hat, but remember that it will take more yarn.

BRIM

Rnd 21: Ch 1, [sc in next st, dc in lower back bar of next st (visible on WS of st)] 28 times, join in first sc.

NUM NUM BIB

This snazzy stain protector is made of lightweight DK washable yarn and is a cute item to pack in your baby supply bag when you go to visit grandma and grandpa. The featured cheery emoji enjoying its dinner will coax your little one to eat up and grow big! Make a week's worth of them in different colors and with different faces as gifts for parents-to-be.

FINISHED MEASUREMENTS
9 inches (23cm) wide by
14 inches (36cm) high

GAUGE
18 sc and 21 sc rows =
4 inches (10cm)

MATERIALS + TOOLS

- DK weight yarn (100% acrylic), 3.5 oz (100g) / 220 yds (200m) per ball, in the following colors:
  - 1 ball, aqua
  - 1 ball, yellow
  - 1 ball, gray
  - 5 yds (4.5m), pink
- 4.25mm hook, or size needed to achieve gauge
- ¾ in. (11mm) snap buttons, 4
- Sharp tapestry needle

Note: Join with sl st unless otherwise indicated.

FRONT

Row 1 (WS): With aqua, ch 30, sc in 2nd ch from hook and in each ch across, turn. (29 sc)

Rows 2–5: 2 sc, 2sc in next st, sc across to last 3 sts, 2sc in next st, 2 sc, turn. (37 sc after row 5)

Rows 6–41: Ch 1, 4 sc, work row 1 of chart, changing colors as necessary, 4 sc, turn.

Rows 42–45: Ch 1, sc in each st across, turn.

NECK SHAPING, FIRST SIDE

Row 1 (RS): Ch 1, 13 sc, dec, turn, leaving rem sts unworked. (14 sts)

Row 2: Ch 1, sk first st, sc in next st and in each st across, turn. (13 sts)

Row 3: Ch 1, sc across to last 2 sts, dec, turn. (12 sts)

Rows 4–5: Rep rows 2–3. (10 sts)

Row 6: Rep row 2. (9 sts)

Rows 7–12: Ch 1, sc across, turn.

Row 13: Ch 1, sc across to last st, 2sc in last st, turn. (10 sc)

Row 14: Ch 1, 1 sc, 2sc in next st, sc across, turn. (11 sc)

Rows 15–18: Rep rows 13–14. (15 sc)

Row 19: Ch 1, sc across, ch 9, turn.

Row 20: Sc in 2nd ch from hook and in next 7 chs, sc across rem sts, turn. (23 sc)

Row 21: Ch 1, sk first st, sc across, turn. (22 sc)

Row 22: Ch 1, sc across to last 2 sts, dec, turn. (21 sc)

Rows 23–24: Rep rows 21–22. (19 sts) Fasten off.

NECK SHAPING, SECOND SIDE

Row 1: With RS facing, sk 7 sts from last st of Neck Shaping, First Side, join (in next st, ch 1, sc in same st as join, sk next st, sc across. (14 sc)

Row 2: Ch 1, sc across to last 2 sts, dec, turn. (13 sc)

Row 3: Ch 1, sk first st, sc across, turn. (12 sc)

Rows 4–5: Rep rows 2–3. (10 sts)

Row 6: Rep row 2. (9 sts)

Rows 7–12: Ch 1, sc across, turn.

Row 13: Ch 1, 1 sc, 2sc in next st, sc across, turn. (10 sc)

Row 14: Ch 1, sc across to last st, 2sc in last st, turn. (11 sc)

Rows 15–18: Rep rows 13–14. (15 sc) Fasten off.

Row 19: With a new slip knot on hook, ch 8, then, beginning in first st of row 18, sc in each st across, turn. (8 chs, 15 sc)

Row 20: Ch 1, sc across, turn. (23 sc)

Row 21: Ch 1, sc across to last 2 sts, dec, turn. (22 sc)

Row 22: Ch 1, sk first st, sc across, turn. (21 sc)

Rows 23–24: Rep rows 21–22. (19 sts) Fasten off.

EDGING

Rnd 1: With yellow, join in any st on back of the neck, ch 1, sc in same st as join, sc evenly around, working 2sc in each corner of back neck strap, in last sc change to gray, sl st in first sc to join.

Rnd 2: Ch 1, sc in same st as join, sc around, working 2 sc in each corner of back neck strap, sl st in first sc to join. Fasten off.

FINISHING

Weave in all ends. Sew or attach snaps to overlapping back neck straps. Steam block with ironing cloth.

Num Num Pattern

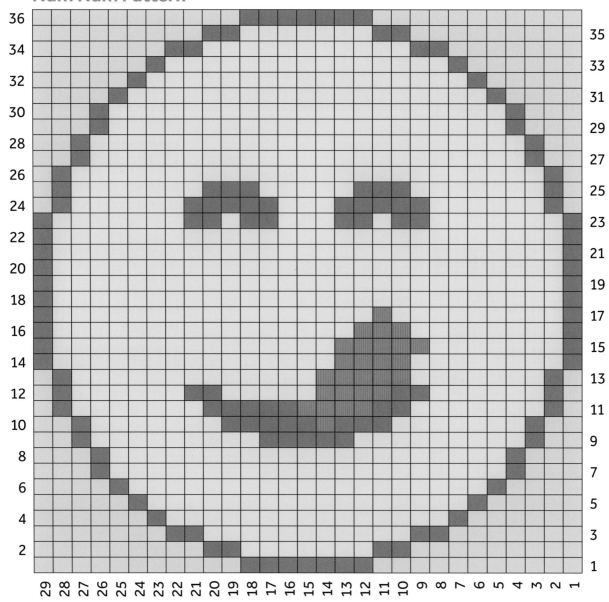

Pattern is not to scale. Refer to instructions for Front on page 69. Colors shown correspond to yarn colors.

Blushing Pattern

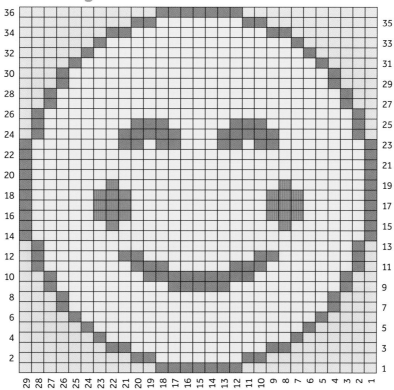

Pattern is not to scale. Colors shown correspond to yarn colors.

Kissing Pattern

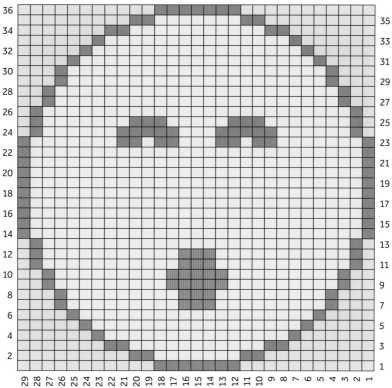

Pattern is not to scale. Colors shown correspond to yarn colors.

Smirking Pattern

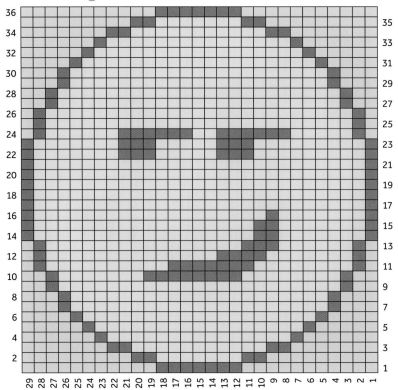

Pattern is not to scale. Colors shown correspond to yarn colors.

Bib Template

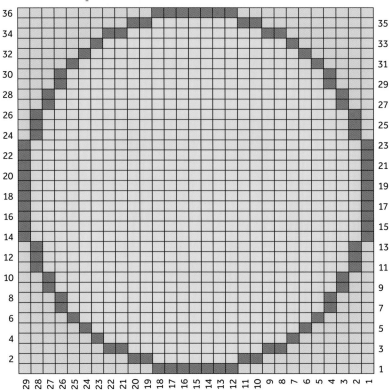

Pattern is not to scale. Colors shown correspond to yarn colors.
Photocopy this template and fill in an emoji design of your choice.

SURLY SLOUCHIE HAT

We all once were one of those moody teenagers who had nothing good to say, or not much to share but a grunt or a scowl. A little sarcasm may bring a smile to the face of your favorite young person with this slouchy hat. Horns are optional. Actually, you can use any of the emoji facial elements from page 16 to give this slouchy a personal touch.

FINISHED MEASUREMENTS
Circumference: 21 inches (53cm)
Brim: 20 inches (50cm)

GAUGE
Worked in the round, 13 hdc = 4 inches (10cm); 11 hdc rnds = 4 inches (10cm)
First 6 rnds of hat = 2 1/4 inches (6cm) in diameter

MATERIALS + TOOLS

- DK weight yarn (70% acrylic, 30% merino wool), 3.5 oz (100g) / 260 yds (238m) per ball, in the following colors:
  - 1 ball, red
  - 1 ball, orange
  - 1 ball, black
- 5.5mm hook or size needed to achieve gauge
- 3.75mm hook or size needed to achieve gauge
- Locking stitch markers
- Less than 1 oz (28g) polyester fiber fill
- Matching sewing thread and needle
- Sharp tapestry needle

SPECIAL STITCHES

Slip stitch cluster (sl-st-cl): Insert hook in first st, yo, pull up lp, insert hook in next st, yo, pull through fabric and lp on hook; *insert hook in same st as last st worked, yo, pull up lp, insert hook in next st, yo, pull through fabric and lp on hook; rep from * around.

Note: Join with sl st unless otherwise indicated

FACIAL FEATURES DIRECTORY

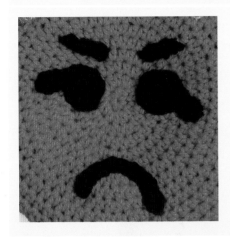

Use the facial elements from Crocheted Facial Features (page 16) to customize your emoji design. Just be sure to use yarn that is the same weight as the rest of your project to keep the face proportional.

Eyes: Side-Looking Eye 1; Side-Looking Eye 2

Mouth: Mouth, Large

Other: Eyebrows, Straight; Horns

CROWN

Rnd 1: With red, work 7 hdc into adjustable ring, join in first hdc. (7 hdc)

Rnd 2: Ch 1, 2hdc in each st around, join in first hdc. (14 hdc)

Rnd 3: Ch 1, [2hdc in next st, hdc in next st] 7 times, join in first hdc. (21 sts)

Rnd 4: Ch 1, [2 hdc, 2hdc in next st] 7 times, join in first hdc. (28 sts)

Rnd 5: Ch 1, [2hdc in next st, hdc in next st] 9 times, hdc in next st, join in first hdc. (37 sts)

Rnd 6: Ch 1, [3 hdc, 2hdc in next st] 9 times, hdc in next st, join in first hdc. (46 sts)

Rnd 7: Ch 1, 2 hdc, [2hdc in next st, 5 hdc] 7 times, 2 hdc, join in first hdc. (53 sts)

Rnd 8: Ch 1, 2 hdc, [4 hdc, 2hdc in next st, 5 hdc] 5 times, 1 hdc, join in first hdc. (58 sts)

Rnd 9: Ch 1, 2 hdc, [2hdc in next st, 8 hdc] 6 times, 2 hdc, join in first hdc. (64 sts)

Rnd 10: Ch 1, 2 hdc, [5 hdc, 2hdc in next st, 4 hdc] 6 times, 2 hdc, join in first hdc. (70 sts)

SIDE

Rnds 11–26: Ch 1, hdc in each st around, making sure to work last hdc in top of sl st of prev rnd and counting every rnd to maintain 70 sts per rnd, join in first hdc.

Work more rows for a deeper slouch, but remember that it will take more yarn.

Place sm in rnds 16 and 23 in a parallel line near joins.

BRIM

Rnd 27 (WS): Turn, sl-st-cl (see Special Stitches) around, sl st in same st as first st, turn.

Rnd 28: Ch 1, sc in back ridge of each st around, join in first sc, turn.

Rnd 29: Sl-st-cl around, sl st in same st as first st, turn.

Rnd 30: Rep rnd 28. Fasten off.

Weave in ends.

Fold so rnd 23 sm is under rnd 16 sm and tack with yarn and tapestry needle to set slouch; remove sms.

FACIAL FEATURES

Create faces using the Facial Features instructions starting on page 16. Mix and match as desired. If you wish to create the face shown in the photographed project, consult the grid at left. Referring to the photographs or according to your own preferences, with sewing thread and needle, attach facial features to project. Stuff horns slightly with fiber fill and with tips turned up, sew in place.

FINISHING

Weave in all ends.

POM-POM BEANIE

Pom-poms are just fun! They are easy to make with all the new tools that are available, but simple cardstock or a cut-up cereal box will work too. I was gifted some pom-pom makers the same week I was swatching for this hat design. I just had to include a pom-pom emoji because it is unique and quirky. Because the face on this hat is made by sewing down pom-poms into the desired pattern, you could create any expression you wish.

FINISHED MEASUREMENTS
Brim circumference:
20 inches (51cm)
Depth: 7 inches (18cm)

GAUGE
14 st = 4 inches (10cm)
12 rnds = 4 inches (10cm)

MATERIALS + TOOLS

- Chunky weight yarn (55% nylon, 45% acrylic), 3.5 oz (100g) / 137 yds (125m) per ball, in the following colors:
  - 1 ball, peach
  - A few yards, black
  - A few yards, red
- 5mm hook or size needed to achieve gauge for ribbing
- 5.5mm hook or size needed to achieve gauge for hat
- 4mm hook for latching
- Pom-pom maker or lightweight cardboard
- 2-in. (5cm)-wide ruler or heavy cardboard strip
- Sharp tapestry needle
- Sewing needle and thread
- Latch hook (optional)

Note: Join with sl st unless otherwise indicated.

SPECIAL STITCHES

Foundation single crochet (fsc): Ch 2, insert hook in first ch and pull up lp, hang open locking sm on yarn, *ch 1 (trapping sm), yo, pull through 2 (sc made), insert hook under front lp of ch and under strand holding sm, yo, pull up lp, move sm to yarn; rep from * until you have the required number of sc. You can stop using the sm once you are familiar with where to insert the hook.

Backward single crochet (bsc): With yarn in front of work, insert hook from back to front under both strands at the top of next st, grab yarn and pull through to the back (2 lps on hook), yo, pull through both lps.

Split single crochet (split sc): The stitch on the current row is worked into the sc in the row below, but instead of going under the 2 top lps as usual, the hook is inserted between the 2 vertical legs of the single crochet to split it; the stitch is then finished as usual.

Decrease (dec): Yo, insert hook under usual top 2 lps of next st, yo, pull up lp, insert hook under 3rd back bar of next st, yo, pull lp through all lps on hook.

BRIM

Row 1: With 5mm hook and peach yarn, fsc (see Special Stitches) 60, turn.

Now working in rounds:

Rnd 1: Ch 1, sc in st at base of ch 1, sc in each st around, join in first sc. After hat is done, close gap with tapestry needle when weaving in ends. (60 sc)

Rnd 2: Ch 1, *split sc (see Special Stitches) in next sc, bsc (see Special Stitches) in next st; rep from * around, join in first sc. (30 split sc, 30 bsc)

Rnd 3: Ch 1, split sc in same sc as join, bsc in next st, *split sc in next st, bsc in next st; rep from * around, join in first st.

Rnds 4–6: Rep rnd 3. More rounds are optional, but be prepared to use more yarn.

SIDES

Rnd 7: Change to 5.5mm hook. Ch 1, hdc in same st as join, hdc in each st around. (60 hdc)

Rnd 8: Ch 1, hdc in same st as join, hdc in 3rd back bar on WS of next hdc (this pushes the top 2 lps toward the RS front of the fabric), *hdc in next st, hdc in 3rd back bar of next st; rep from * around. (30 hdc, 30 back bar-hdc)

Rnds 9–13: Rep rnd 8. More rounds can be worked for a deeper hat, but be prepared to use more yarn.

CROWN

Rnd 14: Ch 1, hdc in same st as join, *[hdc in 3rd back bar of next st, hdc in next st] 3 times, sk next st, dec (see Special Stitches) in next 2 sts, hdc in next st; rep from * 4 more times, rep between [ ] to last st, hdc in 3rd back bar of last st, join in first hdc. (50 sts)

Rnd 15: Rep rnd 8. (25 hdc, 25 back bar hdc)

Rnd 16: Ch 1, hdc in same st as join, *[hdc in 3rd back bar of next st, hdc in next st] 3 times, sk next st, dec in next 2 sts, hdc in next st; rep from * 3 more times, rep between [ ] to last st, hdc in 3rd back bar of last st, join in first hdc. (42 sts)

Rnd 17: Rep rnd 8. (21 hdc, 21 back bar hdc)

Rnd 18: Ch 1, hdc in same st as join, *[hdc in 3rd back bar of next st, hdc in next st] 3 times, sk next st, dec in next 2 sts, hdc in next st; rep from * 3 more times, hdc in 3rd back bar of last st, join in first hdc. (34 sts)

Rnd 19: Rep rnd 8. (17 hdc, 17 back bar hdc)

Rnd 20: Ch 1, hdc in same st as join, *[hdc in 3rd back bar of next st, hdc in next st] 3 times, sk next st, dec in next 2 sts, hdc in next st; rep from * 2 more times, rep between [ ] to last st, hdc in 3rd back bar of last st, join in first hdc. (28 sts)

Rnd 21: Rep rnd 8. (14 hdc, 14 back bar hdc)

Rnd 22: Ch 1, hdc in same st as join, *[hdc in 3rd back bar of next st, hdc in next st] 3 times, sk next st, dec in next 2 sts, hdc in next st; rep from * once, rep between [ ] to last st, hdc in 3rd back bar of last st, join in first hdc. (24 sts)

Rnd 23: Rep rnd 8. (12 hdc, 12 back bar hdc)

Rnd 24: Ch 1, hdc-sc-tog 12 times, join in first st. (12 sts)

Rnd 25: Ch 1, sc2tog 6 times, join in first st. (6 sts)

Cut yarn, leaving a generous tail. With yarn on tapestry needle, weave in and out of front lps of last rnd, pull tight to cinch closed. Push yarn through to inside of hat and weave in end. Weave in end on brim to close gap.

POM-POM FACIAL FEATURES

EYES AND ROSY CHEEKS

Cut 2 cardboard circles that are 1 $\frac{3}{4}$ inches (44mm) in diameter each with a $\frac{3}{8}$-inch (9.5mm) hole in the middle and make 2 black pom-poms as follows:

Cut a 2-yard (1.8m) length of yarn and thread one end through a tapestry or yarn needle. Hold both cardboard circles together and pass the needle and 1 yard of the yarn through the holes. Passing the needle and yarn around the outside edges of the circles, reinsert the needle in the same holes and pull the yarn through. Rep this step until half of the circle is wrapped in yarn. Then use the needle to do the same thing with the other yard of yarn. With sharp, fine-tipped scissors cut between the edges of the cardboard circles and separate the circles from each other by about $\frac{1}{4}$-inch (6mm). Take an 8-inch (20cm) strand of yarn and wrap the strands by placing it between the circles, tightening it, and tying a couple of half-knots. Remove the cardboard circles and brush the pom-pom ends, then trim any extra-long ones. Fuller pom-poms can be made by starting with a longer length of yarn.

Cut 2 circles that are 1 inch (2.5cm) in diameter each with a $\frac{3}{8}$-inch (9.5mm) hole and make 2 red pom-poms. Trim pom-poms to make them neat.

Use the yarn ends from tying the pom-poms to attach eyes and rosy cheeks to hat according to photo. You could also make whatever pom-pom face you choose!

MOUTH

Wrap black yarn around 2-inch (5cm) ruler or card 40 times and cut along one edge of ruler to make mouth strands.

With 5mm hook, ch 18. Fasten off and cut yarn.

With 4mm (or latch) hook, fold 1 strand around hook and hold in place, insert hook in top lp of first ch, wrap both ends of strand over hook and pull both ends through ch and through lp on hook. Rep with remaining strands across all back lps of next 17 chs. Then rotate and rep across front lps of all 18 chs. Trim ends of latched strand to $\frac{1}{2}$-inch (13mm). Arrange mouth on hat referring to photo and sew with sewing thread and needle along both edges of chain with latched knots.

KISSY POCKET SCARF

Crochet has endless combinations of stitches and stitch blends and shapes, and so many stitches or stitch patterns are given names because of what they resemble, like shells and fans. This scarf features a stitch-blend I invented called the tilted-A stitch because of its triangular shape and the horizontal strands of yarn that cross its middle. The end result is a new lacy stitch pattern that could be used for many other projects. Try this stitch for a baby blanket or a poncho! The emoji pockets on this scarf are the perfect addition to keep the wearer's hands warm. Use any emoji facial elements from page 16 to make this scarf your own design.

FINISHED MEASUREMENTS
8 inches (20 cm) wide by
60 inches (152cm) long

GAUGE
In tilted-A pattern: 6 rows and
7 sts = 4 inches (10cm)

MATERIALS + TOOLS

- DK weight yarn (100% acrylic), 1.75 oz (50g) / 161 yds (147m) per ball, in the following colors:
  - 3 balls, blue
  - 3 balls, pink
  - 3 balls, white
  - 1 ball, yellow
  - 1 ball, black
  - 1 ball, red
- 5mm hook or size needed to achieve gauge
- Sewing needle and matching sewing thread
- Sharp tapestry needle

FACIAL FEATURES DIRECTORY

Use the facial elements from Crocheted Facial Features (page 16) to customize your emoji design. Just be sure to use yarn that is the same weight as the rest of your project to keep the face proportional.

Eyes: Oval Eye, Medium
Mouth: Smoochy Lips, Large
Other: Hearts, Medium

STRIPE SEQUENCE

12 blue rows, *3 pink rows, 5 white rows, 3 pink rows**, 5 blue rows; rep from * ending at ** when scarf measures approximately 55 inches (140cm), work last 12 rows in blue.

SCARF

With blue, ch 30, sc in 2nd ch from hook and in each ch across. (29 sc)

Row 1: Ch 3, dc in st at base of ch-3, ch 1, dc2tog with first leg in same st, sk 1 st and work 2nd leg in next st, *ch 1, dc2tog with first leg in same st, sk 1 st, and work 2nd leg in next st; rep from *across, ch 1, dc in last st, turn. (2 dc, 14 dc2tog)

Row 2: Ch 2, dc in st at base of ch-2, [ch 1, t-A st (see page 10)] across to last st, ch 1, dc2tog in last t-A st made and last st, turn. (15 t-A sts)

Rows 3–12: Rep row 2 to last dc2tog of row 12. Work dc2tog until there are 3 lps on hook and then yo with the next color in the stripe sequence and pull through 3 lps on hook.

Rep row 2 and continue changing colors this way according to Stripe Sequence until scarf measures approximately 55 inches (140cm), then work last 12 rows in blue.

Last row: Ch 1, sc 29 evenly across. Fasten off.

Weave in ends.

FACE

Rnd 1: With yellow, make an adjustable ring and ch 1, work 10 hdc into ring, sl st in top of first hdc to join. (10 hdc)

Rnd 2: Ch 2 (does not count as st here and throughout), 2 dc in each hdc around, sl st in top of first dc to join. (20 dc)

Rnd 3: Ch 2, [hdc in next st, 2 hdc in next st] around, sl st in top of first hdc to join. (30 hdc)

Rnd 4: Ch 2, 2 dc in each of first 2 sts, dc in next st, [2 dc in next st, dc in next 2 sts] around, sl st in top of first dc to join. (41 dc)

Rnd 5: Ch 2, [hdc in next st, 2 hdc in next st, hdc in next 2 sts] 10 times, hdc in each rem st around, sl st in top of first hdc to join. (51 hdc)

Rnd 6: Ch 2, 2 dc in each of first 2 sts, [dc in next 4 sts, 2 dc in next st] 9 times, dc in each rem st around, sl st in top of first dc to join. (62 dc)

Rnd 7: Ch 2, [hdc in next 5 sts, 2 hdc in next st] 10 times, hdc in each rem st around, sl st in top of first hdc to join. (72 hdc)

Rnd 8: Ch 2, 2 dc in each of first 2 sts, [dc in next 6 sts, 2 dc in next st] 9 times, dc in each rem st around, sl st in top of first dc to join. (83 dc)

Rnd 9: Ch 2, hdc in next 3 sts, 2 hdc in each of next 2 sts, [hdc in next 7 sts, 2 hdc in next st] 9 times, hdc in each rem st around, sl st in top of first hdc to join. (94 hdc)

Rnd 10: Ch 1, sc in same st as join, sc in next 14 sts, 2 sc in next st, [14 sc, 2sc in next st] 5 times, sc in each rem st.

Fasten off. Close with sewn invisible join (see page 13).

FACIAL FEATURES

Create faces using the Facial Features instructions starting on page 16. Mix and match as desired. If you wish to create the faces shown in the photographed project, consult the grid above. Referring to the photographs or according to your own preferences, with sewing thread and needle, attach facial features to project. Sew each face onto scarf ends, leaving a 4-inch (10cm) opening at the top of each face pocket.

NOT TOO BLUE FOR YOU MITTENS

Everyone knows that chilly winds and snow make for some pretty blue fingers that sting or ache with cold. These mitts will take those blues away and put a smile on your face. Your fingers will be snuggled up together in one warm wooly place, and if you need to, you can even tuck your thumb in, too. Add a smiley emoji to warm up someone else's day—or embroider a grimacing face if you want some sympathy. Because the emoji faces on these mittens are embroidered on, it's easy to create whatever design you like to show how you feel about winter's arrival.

FINISHED MEASUREMENTS
Length: 7 (9, 9¾) inches (18 [23, 25cm])
Circumference: 5½ (6¼, 7) inches (14 [16, 18cm])

GAUGE
Slanted Stocking Pattern: 18 sts and 9 rows = 4 inches (10cm)

 or

MATERIALS + TOOLS

- Light worsted weight yarn (100% superwash wool), 3.5 oz (100g) / 220 yds (200m) per ball, in the following color:
    - 1 ball, dark blue
    - 1 ball, speckled blue
    - A few yards, navy blue
- 4mm hook or size needed to achieve gauge
- Sharp tapestry needle

SPECIAL STITCHES

Extended single crochet (e-sc): Insert hook into indicated st, yo, pull up lp, ch 1, yo, pull through 2 lps on hook.

Split single crochet (split sc): Refers to the sc stitch you are inserting the hook into to make the indicated st. Below the 2 top strands, divide the 2 vertical strands of the sc as if piercing the heart of the st.

Note: Join with sl st unless otherwise indicated. Sizes given are small, medium, and large. Instructions are given with small first and medium and large within parentheses.

SLANTED STOCKING PATTERN

Even round: Ch 1, sc in each st around, join in first st with sl st (with splitting sts below).

Odd round: Ch 1, e-sc in split sc around, join in first st with sl st.

Rep these 2 rnds for established pattern.

CUFF

Make 2.

Set-up: With dark blue, ch 5, remove hook from lp, insert hook through front of first ch to back and allow to rest higher up the shank, return live lp to hook, ch 24 (28, 32). Pull live lp through st higher on shank to join in the round.

Rnd 1: Ch 1, sc in same st as join, dc in next st, [sc in next st, dc in next st] around, join in top of first sc.

Rnd 2: Ch 1, [sc in split sc (see Special Stitches), fpdc around next dc] around, join in first sc with sl st.

Rnd 3: Ch 1, [sc in split sc, fpdc around next fpdc] around, join in first sc with sl st.

Rnds 4–7 (4–8, 4–9): Rep rnd 3.

THUMB GUSSET

Rnd 1: Ch 1, [1 e-sc (see Special Stitches) in split sc, 2e-sc in next fpdc] 8 (10, 10) times, e-sc in each rem st, join in first sc. (32 [38, 42] sts)

Rnd 2: Ch 1, sc in each st around, join in first st with sl st (with splitting sts below).

Rnd 3: Ch 1, e-sc in split sc around, join in first st with sl st.

Rnds 4–8 (4–10, 4–10): Rep rnds 2–3 for Slanted Stocking Pattern.

LEFT HAND

Rnd 1: Sc in next 10 (10, 12) sts, change color to speckled blue yarn in last sc, 2sc in next st, sc in next 20 (26, 28) sts, 2sc in next st, ch 2, skipping all first sts in prev color, join in first new color sc with sl st. (24 [30, 32] sts and 2 chs)

Rnd 2: Ch 1, e-sc in next split sc around to 2 chs, e-sc in each ch. (26 [32, 34] sts)

Rnds 3–10 (3–11, 3–12): Continue in established Slanted Stocking Pattern.

FINGER TIP

Rnd 1: Ch 1, sc in next 3 (4, 5) sts, [dec in next 2 sts] twice, sc in next 9 (12, 13) sts, [dec in next 2 sts] twice, sc in each rem st, join in first sc. (22 [28, 30] sts)

Rnd 3: Ch 1, sc in next 2 (3, 4) sts, [dec in next 2 sts] twice, sc in next 7 (10, 11) sts, [dec in next 2 sts] twice, sc in each rem st, join in first sc. (18 [24, 26] sts)

Rnd 4: Ch 1, sc in next 1 (2, 3) st(s), [dec in next 2 sts] twice, sc in next 5 (8, 9) sts, [dec in next 2 sts] twice, sc in each rem st, join in first sc. (14 [20, 22] sts)

Small Size Only

Skip to Finishing.

Other Sizes

Rnd 5: Ch 1, sc in next (1, 2) st(s), [dec in next 2 sts] twice, sc in next (6, 7) sts, [dec in next 2 sts] twice, sc in each rem st, join in first sc. ([16, 18] sts)

Medium Size Only

Skip to Finishing.

Large Size Only

Rnd 6: Ch 1, sc in next (1) st, [dec in next 2 sts] twice, sc in next (6, 7) sts, [dec in next 2 sts] twice, sc in each rem st, join in first sc. ([14] sts)

Go to Finishing.

RIGHT HAND

Rnd 1: Fasten off. Join speckled blue yarn in 2nd st from join, ch 1, 2sc in same st as join, sc in next 20 (26, 28) sts, 2sc in next st, ch 2, skipping all rem sts, join in first new color sc with sl st. (24 [30, 32] sts)

Rnd 2: Ch 1, e-sc in next split sc around to 2 chs, e-sc in each ch. (26 [32, 34] sts)

Rnds 3–10 (3–11, 3–12): Continue in established Slanted Stocking Pattern.

FINGER TIP

Work as for Left Mitten.

FINISHING

Fasten off. Turn mitten inside out. With tapestry needle, whip stitch the opening at the top closed and weave in ends. Return mitten right side out.

THUMB

Rnd 1: With dark blue, in opposite side of 2nd ch made in Thumb Gusset, join. Work 1 rnd of e-sc around, join in first sc with sl st. (12 [12, 14] sts)

Rnd 2: Ch 1, [sc in next st, dec in next 2 sts] 3 (2, 2) times, sc in rem sts, join in first sc with sl st. (9 [10, 12] sts)

Work in established Slanted Stocking Pattern for 4 (6, 6) more rows.

Rnd 7 (9, 9): Ch 1, [dec in next 2 sts] 4 (5, 6) times, sc in any rem sts, join in first sc with sl st.

Rnd 8 (10, 10): Ch 1, sc in each st around. Fasten off.

With tapestry needle, weave in and out of front lps only of all sts and pull closed. Push needle through partway and turn mitten inside out to weave in ends.

FACIAL FEATURE EMBROIDERY

With navy blue, embroider the face. You can make the face shown in the photos, or create your own. Use a double running stitch (page 15) to make an outline of a circle and desired facial features.

SMELLY SLIPPERS

These toe-up foot warmers are fun, fast, and fabulous gifts to make for others to keep their feet toasty warm. Embroider a nauseated face on slippers for someone whose feet you generally don't want to see . . . or smell. Or put a cheery emoji on a pair for someone who's feeling down. Whichever emoji you choose to add to the yellow face you crochet into the toe, it'll be a great token of your affection for the recipient.

FINISHED MEASUREMENTS
Length: 9 to 10 inches
(23 to 25cm)

GAUGE
13 hdc and 11.5 hdc rounds =
4 inches (10cm)

MEDIUM

MATERIALS + TOOLS

- Worsted weight yarn (100% acrylic), 7 oz (197g) / 275 yds (251m) per ball, in the following colors:
  - 1 ball, green
  - 1 ball, yellow
  - 1 ball, black
  - 1 ball, red
- 4.5mm hook or size needed to achieve gauge
- Stitch markers
- Sharp tapestry needle

SPECIAL STITCHES

Increase (inc): Sc in blo of indicated st, sc in both lps of same st.

Blended decrease (bdec): Yo, insert hook in next st, yo, pull up lp, insert hook in next st, yo, pull through all lps on hook.

Invisible decrease (invdec): Yo, insert hook under flo of next st, insert hook immediately into next st, yo, draw lp through fabric and first lp on hook (3 lps rem on hook), yo, draw through rem 3 lps.

PATTERN NOTES

■ Place a sm in the last st of the rnd. On following rnds, after working into marked st, move sm up to st just made.

■ To change color, work last hdc in current color until there are 3 lps on the hook, yo with the new color, leaving a 4-inch (10 cm) tail, and draw through 3 lps on hook.

■ To carry the main color behind the face sts, work over the strand of yarn only every third st in the contrasting face color, and carry loosely at the back to avoid puckering.

TOE

We'll begin by working into both sides of the starting chain (see page 12).

Rnd 1: With green, ch 6, 2sc in blo of 2nd ch from hook, sc in blo of next 3 sts, 2sc in blo of last ch, 1 more sc in same st on far side of knot, sc in opposite side of next 3 chs, 2sc in back strand of next ch, place sm in last st made to indicate last st of rnd. (12 sc)

Rnd 2: Inc (see Special Stitches) in first 2 sts, 3 sc, inc in each of next 3 sts, 4 sc, inc in last st. (19 sc)

Rnd 3: Sc in each st around.

Rnd 4: Sc in first 2 sts, inc in next st, 6 sc, inc, 1 sc, inc, 6 sc, inc. (23 sts)

Rnd 5: 1 sc, inc, 8 sc, inc, 1 sc, inc, 10 sc. (26 sts)

Rnd 6: 1 sc, inc, 10 sc, inc in each of next 2 sts, 11 sc, inc. (30 sts)

Rnd 7: 1 sc, inc, 14 sc, inc, 13 sc. (32 sts)

Rnd 8: 32 hdc, removing sm from last hdc worked, 2 more hdc, replace sm in last hdc made (this shifts the start of the round).

Rnd 9: 33 hdc (shifts round by 1 more st).

Rnd 10: 32 hdc.

FACE

The beginning of the round shifts past the sm in some instances; simply move the sm to the last st of each rnd of instructions.

Rnd 11: 5 hdc, change to yellow, 6 hdc in yellow, trapping green underneath every third st (see Pattern Notes), 2 hdc in next st, changing to green in 2nd one, cut yellow yarn, leaving a 4-inch (10cm) tail, 1 hdc in green, 1 bdec (see Special Stitches), 18 hdc. (8 yellow sts, 24 green sts)

Rnd 12: In green 4 hdc, in yellow 9 hdc (trapping green), in green 20 hdc, cut yellow yarn. (9 yellow sts, 23 green sts)

Rnd 13: In green 4 hdc, in yellow 9 hdc (trapping green), 2 hdc in next st, in green 1 hdc, 1 bdec, 16 hdc, cut yellow yarn. (11 yellow sts, 21 green sts)

Rnd 14: In green 3 hdc, in yellow 11 hdc (trapping green), 2 hdc in next st, in green 1 hdc, 1 bdec, 15 hdc, cut yellow yarn. (13 yellow sts, 19 green sts)

Rnd 15: In green 1 hdc, (1 green hdc and 1 yellow hdc) in next st, 13 yellow hdc, 17 green hdc. (14 yellow sts, 18 green sts)

Rnd 16: In green 1 hdc, (1 green hdc and 1 yellow hdc) in next st, in yellow, 1 hdc, 1 invdec (see Special Stitches), 9 hdc, 2 hdc in next st, 18 green hdc. (14 yellow sts, 19 green sts)

Rnd 17: In green, 2 hdc, in yellow, 1 hdc, 1 invdec, 10 hdc, in green, 18 hdc. (12 yellow sts, 20 green sts)

Rnd 18: In green, 2 hdc, 2 hdc in next st, in yellow, 1 hdc, 1 invdec, 8 hdc, in green, 20 hdc. (10 yellow sts, 22 green sts)

Rnd 19: In green, 2 hdc, 2 hdc in next st, in yellow, 1 hdc, 1 invdec, 6 hdc, in green, 21 hdc. (8 yellow sts, 24 green sts)

Rnd 20: 32 hdc.

Rnd 30: 33 hdc.

Rnd 31: 38 hdc, turn.

FOOT OPENING

Now working in rows.

Row 1: Ch 1, 21 hdc, turn, leaving rem sts unworked.

Rows 2–11: Ch 1, 21 hdc, turn.

Work fewer or more rows to adjust size.

HEEL

Ch 1, 9 hdc, 1 invdec, fold work in half, WS tog, insert hook through back lp of first st on front layer and front lp of first st on back layer, yo, pull through all lps on hook, *insert hook through back lp of next st on front layer and front lp of first st on back layer, yo, pull through all lps on hook; rep from * across.

OPENING

Ch 1, sc evenly around opening, work sewn invisible join (see page 13).

Weave in ends.

FACIAL FEATURE EMBROIDERY

With black and red, embroider facial features. You can make the face shown in the photos, or create your own. Use a double running stitch (page 15) to make an outline around the shape you choose to include. To fill the shape, use long and short satin stitches (page 15). These consist of lines that are tightly placed parallel to each other to fill in the gap. The insertion and exit points of the tapestry needle do not have to line up; in fact, staggering them is better and gives a more solid look to the shape.

BIG GRIN HOODIE

This comfortable hoodie comes in a range of sizes so that you can make a set for a family or a coordinating pair for a couple. Use the blank template to draw your own emoji to customize the hoodie or select from the several that are provided. Using a lightweight yarn is key to keeping this hoodie looking great, with a casual flow to the fabric and a relaxed fit.

FINISHED MEASUREMENTS

Chest: 23 (27, 31, 32, 36, 40, 44, 48, 52, 56) inches (58 [69, 79, 81, 91, 112, 122, 132, 142cm])

GAUGE

See Gauge Swatch (page 92)

MATERIALS + TOOLS

- DK weight yarn (55% superwash merino wool/45% acrylic), 3.5 oz (100g) / 273 yds (250m) per ball, in the following colors:
  - Yellow, see table below for quantity
  - Green, see table below for quantity
  - 1 ball, brown
  - 1 ball, white
- 4.25mm hook or size needed to achieve gauge
- Locking stitch markers, 2 unique colors
- Half capful, gentle shampoo
- Warm water and basin
- Towels

BALLS OF YARN NEEDED

	CHILD SIZES			ADULT SIZES						
	2	6	12	XS	S	M	L	1X	2X	3X
Yellow	1	1	1	1	1	1	1	2	2	2
Green	3	4	5	6	6	7	8	9	10	10

Note: Included sizes are child's sizes 2 (6, 12) and adult sizes (XS, S, M, L, 1X, 2X, 3X). Instructions are given for child's size 2, with larger sizes appearing in ( ). Join with sl st unless otherwise indicated.

SPECIAL STITCHES

Decrease (dec): Insert hook in back lp of next st, yo, pull up lp, insert hook in front lp of next st, yo, pull yarn through all lps on hook.

GAUGE SWATCH

Row 1: Ch 24, hdc in 2nd ch from hook and in each ch across. (23 hdc)

Row 2: Ch 1, extend lp, hdc across, turn.

Rows 3–23: Rep row 2.

Swatch should measure 6½ inches (17cm) wide and 7 inches (18cm) tall.

14 hdc and 13.25 hdc rows per 4 inches (10cm).

PATTERN NOTES

- Wind balls of small quantities (20 g) of yarn as follows:
  4 balls of brown
  1 ball of white
  3 balls of yellow
  1 ball of green

- Ch 1 at beginning of rows should be worked loosely. The last hdc of every row goes into the 2 strands of this ch-1, which lie slightly to the back of the last st of each row.

- The chart is worked across the center stitches and rows of the Back. There are rows before and after and stitches on either side which form a frame for the chart.

- Do not carry color under stitches and do not tie knots to add new color; join a new ball of yarn as indicated in the instructions, leaving a 5-inch (13cm) tail to weave in.

- When working Hoodie Short Rows, move sms up each row into the st that was worked into a marked st unless otherwise stated.

BACK

Row 1: With green, ch 41 (49, 55, 57, 65, 71, 79, 85, 93, 101) hdc in 2nd ch from hook and in each ch across, turn. (40 [48, 54, 56, 64, 70, 78, 84, 92, 100] hdc)

Row 2: Ch 1, extend lp, hdc in each st across, turn.

SIZE 2 ONLY

Skip to Child Size Emoji Chart.

ALL OTHER SIZES

Rows 3–6 (16, 16, 16, 20, 20, 18, 18, 20): Rep row 2. All adult sizes, skip to Adult-Size Emoji Chart.

CHILD-SIZE EMOJI CHART

Sizes 2, 6, 12 only (work the Toothy Grin, Small pattern, page 96).

Row 1: Ch 1, work 3 (7, 10) hdc in green for frame, begin row 1 on grid from right to left as follows: 10 green hdc, with green, yo, insert hook in next st, yo, pull up lp (3 green lps on hook), with brown (leaving a 5-inch [13cm] tail), yo, pull through all lps on hook, bring green yarn between hook and brown yarn, to front of work facing you (color change complete), 11 brown hdc, with brown, yo, insert hook in next st, yo, pull up lp (3 brown lps on hook), with green (leaving a 5-inch [13cm] tail), yo, pull through all lps on hook, bring brown yarn between hook and green yarn to front of work facing you, 11 green hdc for remainder of chart, 3 (7, 10) hdc in green for frame, turn.

Row 2: Ch 1, work 3 (7, 10) hdc in green for frame, begin row 2 on grid from left to right as follows: 8 green hdc, with green, yo, insert hook in next st, yo, pull up lp, with brown, yo, pull through all lps on hook, bring green to front of work, trapping extra strand of brown created across wrong side of work under next 2 sts, work 1 brown hdc in next st, with brown, yo, insert hook in next st, yo, pull up lp, with yellow (leaving a 5-inch [13cm] tail), yo, pull through all lps on hook, bring brown to front of work, 11 yellow hdc, with yellow, yo, insert hook in next st, yo, pull up lp, with brown (leaving a 5-inch [13cm] tail), yo, pull through all lps on hook, bring yellow to front of work, trapping green under next 2 sts, work 1 brown hdc, with brown, yo, insert hook in next st, yo, pull up lp, with green, yo, pull through all lps on hook, bring brown to front, 9 green hdc, work rem sts in green hdc for frame, turn.

Row 3: Ch 1, work 3 (7, 10) hdc in green for frame, begin row 3 on grid from right to left as follows: 7 green hdc changing to brown in last st, bring green to front of work between hook and brown yarn, trapping extra strand of brown, work 2 brown hdc changing to yellow in 2nd st, bring brown to front between hook and yellow yarn, trapping extra strand of yellow, work 2 yellow hdc, 12 more yellow hdc changing to brown in 2nd st, bring yellow to front between hook and brown yarn, trapping green work 2 brown hdc changing to green in 2nd st, bring brown to front between hook and green yarn, work green hdc across rem sts.

Row 4: Ch 1, work 3 (7, 10) hdc in green for frame, begin row 4 on grid from left to right as follows: 6 green hdc changing to brown in last st, bring green to front of work between hook and brown yarn, trapping extra strand of brown, work 1 brown hdc changing to yellow, bring brown to front between hook and yellow yarn, trapping extra strand of yellow, work 2 yellow hdc, 17 more yellow hdc, with brown, yo, insert hook in next st, with, yo, pull up lp, yo, draw through all 3 lps on hook, bring yellow to front of work between hook and brown yarn (color change on the chart square with the diagonal line across it now complete, top of stitch is yellow, bottom of stitch is brown), 1 brown hdc changing to green, bring brown yarn to front of work between hook and green yarn, hdc in green across rem sts.

Next 12 (14, 16) rows: Continue with 3 (7, 10) green, hdc on each side of chart grid and working back and forth across chart rows, changing colors as established with last yo and pull through in the new color and trapping extra strands of yarn. Remember to bring the former color forward to the front of work between the hook and the new color after the color change has been worked. When you encounter the diagonal line in a chart square, in the new color work the yo before you insert the hook.

ADULT-SIZE EMOJI CHART

Sizes XS to 3X only (work the Toothy Grin, Large pattern, page 97).

Row 1: Ch 1, work (6, 10, 13, 17, 20, 24, 28) hdc in green for frame, begin row 1 on grid from right to left as follows: 17 hdc in green, with green, yo, insert hook in next st, yo, pull up lp (3 green lps on hook), with brown (leaving a 5-inch [13cm] tail), yo, pull through all lps on hook, bring green yarn between hook and brown yarn, to front of work facing you (color change complete), 8 brown hdc, with brown, yo, insert hook in next st, yo, pull up lp (3 brown lps on hook), with green (leaving a 5-inch [13cm] tail), yo, pull through all lps on hook, bring brown yarn between hook and green yarn, to front of work facing you, 17 green hdc for remainder of chart, (6, 10, 13, 17, 20, 24, 28) hdc in green for frame, turn.

Row 2: Ch 1, work (6, 10, 13, 17, 20, 24, 28) hdc in green for frame, begin row 2 on grid from left to right as follows: 12 green hdc, with green, yo, insert hook in next st, yo, pull up lp, with brown, yo, pull through all lps on hook, bring green to front of work, trapping extra strand of brown created across wrong side of work under next 4 sts, with brown, yo, insert hook in next st, yo, pull up lp, with yellow (leaving a 5-inch [13cm] tail), yo, pull through all lps on hook, bring brown to front of work, 6 yellow hdc, with yellow, yo, insert hook in next st, yo, pull up lp, with brown (leaving a 5-inch [13cm] tail), yo, pull through all lps on hook, bring yellow to front of work, work 1 brown hdc, trapping green under next 4 sts, work 3 brown hdc, with brown, yo, insert hook in next st, yo, pull up lp, with green, yo, pull through all lps on hook, bring brown to front, 14 green hdc, work rem sts in green hdc for frame, turn.

Row 3: Ch 1, work (6, 10, 13, 17, 20, 24, 28) hdc in green for frame, begin row 3 on grid from right to left as follows: 12 green hdc changing to brown in last st,

bring green to front of work between hook and brown yarn, trapping extra strand of brown, work 3 brown hdc changing to yellow in 3rd st, bring brown to front between hook and yellow yarn, trapping extra strand of yellow, work 4 yellow hdc, 9 more yellow hdc, trapping brown work 2 more yellow hdc changing to brown in 2nd st, bring yellow to front between hook and brown yarn, trapping green work 3 brown hdc changing to green in 3rd st, bring brown to front between hook and green yarn, work green hdc across rem sts.

Row 4: Ch 1, work (6, 10, 13, 17, 20, 24, 28) hdc in green for frame, begin row 4 on grid from left to right as follows: 9 green hdc changing to brown in last st, bring green to front of work between hook and brown yarn, trapping extra strand of brown, work 3 brown hdc changing to yellow, bring brown to front between hook and yellow yarn, trapping extra strand of yellow, work 2 yellow hdc, 15 more yellow hdc, trapping strand of brown, work 2 more yellow hdc, changing to brown in last one, 4 brown hdc changing to green in last one, bring brown yarn to front of work between hook and green yarn, hdc in green across rem sts.

Next (28, 26, 26, 26, 28, 28, 24) rows: Continue with (6, 10, 13, 17, 20, 24, 28) green hdc on each side of chart grid and working back and forth across chart rows, changing colors as established with last yo and pull through in the new color and trapping extra strands of yarn. Remember to bring the former color forward to the front of work between the hook and the new color after the color change has been worked.

ARMHOLE SHAPING

Sizes 2 (6, 12, XS, S, M) Only

Row 1: Ch 1, hdc in first st, dec (see Special Stitches) in next 2 sts, continue in pattern as established across to last 3 sts, dec in next 2 sts, hdc in last st, turn. (38 [46, 52, 54, 62, 68] sts)

Row 2: Ch 1, work in established pattern across, turn.

Rep last 2 rows 3 (5, 6, 3, 5, 6) times. (32 [36, 40, 48, 52, 56] sts)

Next Row: Ch 1, hdc across, turn.

Continue even in hdc rows working any chart rows necessary and in plain green once chart rows are finished until length from start of Armhole Shaping measures 4¾ (5½, 7, 7, 7½, 8) inches (12 [14, 18, 18, 19, 20cm]).

SIZES (L, 1X, 2X, 3X) ONLY

Row 1: Ch 1, hdc in first st, dec (see Special Stitches) in next 2 sts, continue in pattern as established across to last 3 sts, dec in next 2 sts, hdc in last st, turn. ([76, 82, 90, 98] sts)

Rep row 1 (7, 11, 14, 16) times. ([62, 60, 62, 66] sts)

Next Row: Ch 1, hdc across, turn.

Continue even in hdc rows working any chart rows necessary and in plain green once chart rows are finished until length from start of Armhole Shaping measures (8½, 9, 9½, 10) inches (22, 23, 24, 25cm).

FRONT POCKET

Row 1: With green, ch 41 (49, 55, 57, 65, 71, 79, 85, 93, 101), hdc in 2nd ch from hook and in each ch across, turn. (40 [48, 54, 56, 64, 70, 78, 84, 92, 100] hdc)

Rows 2–3 (5, 12, 14, 13, 13, 13, 11, 12, 11): Ch 1, hdc in each st across, turn.

Decrease row 1: Ch 1, hdc in first st, dec in next 2 sts, hdc across to last 3 sts, dec in next 2 sts, hdc in last st, turn. (38 [46, 52, 54, 62, 68, 76, 82, 90, 98] hdc)

Decrease row 2: Ch 1, hdc in first st, dec in next 2 sts, hdc in next st, dec in next 2 sts, hdc across to last 6 sts, dec in next 2 sts, hdc in next st, dec in next 2 sts, hdc in last st, turn. (34 [42, 48, 50, 58, 64, 72, 78, 86, 94] hdc)

[Rep Decrease rows 1–2] 3 (4, 5, 5, 5, 6, 7, 8, 9, 9) times. (16 [18, 18, 20, 28, 28, 30, 30, 32, 40] sts)

[Rep Decrease row 1] 1 (1, 0, 0, 0, 1, 0, 1, 0, 0) times. (14 [16, 18, 20, 28, 26, 30, 28, 32, 40] sts)

[Rep Decrease row 2] 0 (0, 0, 0, 1, 0, 1, 0, 0, 1) times. (14 [16, 18, 20, 24, 26, 26, 28, 32, 36] sts) Fasten off.

FRONT

Row 1: With green, ch 41 (49, 55, 57, 65, 71, 79, 85, 93, 101), hdc in 2nd ch from hook and in each ch across, turn. (40 [48, 54, 56, 64, 70, 78, 84, 92, 100] hdc)

Rows 2–12 (16, 24, 26, 28, 28, 30, 30, 32, 32): Ch 1, hdc in each st across, turn.

Next row: Ch 1, hdc in first 13 (16, 18, 18, 20, 22, 26, 28, 30, 32) sts, place WS of Front Pocket over RS of Front, working through both layers, hdc across next 14 (16, 18, 20, 24, 26, 26, 28, 32, 36) sts to join Front Pocket to Front, hdc across rem sts of Front.

Next row: Ch 1, hdc in each st across, turn.

Rep last row until Front from starting ch is the same length as the Back to the beginning of Armhole Shaping, ending with a WS row.

ARMHOLE SHAPING

Work first 6 (6, 8, 8, 8, 10, 10, 10, 12, 12) rows of Armhole Shaping as for Back.

Find center 8 (8, 10, 12, 12, 12, 12, 12, 12, 12) sts and mark first and last st of these center sts.

LEFT SIDE

Continue working Armhole Shaping as for Back and at the same time, at inner left edge that begins in st before first marked st, decrease 1 st every 1 (1, 2, 1, 1, 1, 1, 1, 1, 1) row(s) 2 (2, 8, 4, 2, 4, 4, 4, 4, 2) times, then at inner left edge, decrease 1 st

every 2 (2, 3, 2, 2, 2, 2, 2, 2, 2) rows 4 (5, 0, 6, 8, 7, 7, 8, 8, 10) times. (6 [7, 7, 8, 10, 11, 14, 12, 13, 15] sts)

Work even in hdc rows until Front Armhole measures the same as Back Armhole. Fasten off.

RIGHT SIDE

Join yarn with sl st in first st after 2nd marked center st. Continue working Armhole Shaping as for Back and at the same time, at inner right edge that begins in st before first marked st, decrease 1 st every 1 (1, 2, 1, 1, 1, 1, 1, 1, 1) row(s) 2 (2, 8, 4, 2, 4, 4, 4, 4, 2) times, then at inner right edge, decrease 1 st every 2 (2, 3, 2, 2, 2, 2, 2, 2, 2) rows 4 (5, 0, 6, 8, 7, 7, 8, 8, 10) times. (6 [7, 7, 8, 10, 11, 14, 12, 13, 15] sts)

Work even in hdc rows until Front Armhole measures the same as Back Armhole. Fasten off.

SLEEVES

Make 2.

Row 1: With green, ch 17 (19, 21, 25, 27, 29, 31, 33, 33, 35), hdc in 2nd ch from hook and in each ch across, turn. (16 [18, 20, 24, 26, 28, 30, 32, 32, 34] hdc)

Row 2: Ch 1, sc in flo across, turn.

Row 3 (increase row): Ch 1, hdc in next st, 2 hdc in next st, hdc across to last 2 sts, 2 hdc in next st, hdc in last st, turn. (18 [20, 22, 26, 28, 30, 32, 34, 34, 36] hdc)

Next 5 (6, 7, 6, 6, 6, 7, 9, 4, 14) rows: Ch 1, hdc across, turn.

Rep last 6 (7, 8, 7, 7, 7, 8, 10, 5, 15) rows 2 (1, 0, 1, 1, 1, 1, 3, 11, 3) times. (22 [22, 22, 28, 30, 32, 34, 40, 56, 42] sts)

Next row: Rep row 3.

Next 4 (5, 6, 8, 8, 8, 7, 5, 0, 3) rows: Ch 1, hdc across, turn.

Rep last 5 (6, 7, 9, 9, 9, 8, 6, 0, 4) rows 1 (3, 5, 3, 3, 3, 4, 4, 0, 9) times. (26 [30, 34, 36, 38, 40, 44, 50, 58, 62] hdc)

Work even in hdc rows until Sleeve measures 8½ (11½, 15, 16½, 17, 17 ½, 17½, 18, 18) inches (22 [29, 38, 42, 43, 43, 44, 44, 46, 46cm]) from cuff.

SHAPE SLEEVE CAP

Decrease 1 st each side of Sleeve every 1 (2, 2, 1, 2, 2, 2, 4, 4, 5) rows 3 times. (20 [24, 28, 30, 32, 36, 38, 44, 52, 56] hdc) Fasten off.

HOOD

Sew shoulder seams of Front and Back.

Row 1: With RS facing, join in first st at back neck opening and work 20 (22, 26, 32, 32, 34, 34, 36, 36, 36) hdc evenly across, turn.

Rows 2–8: Ch 1, hdc across, turn.

Place unique color sm in each end of last row worked; do not move.

Rows 9–16 (16, 18, 18, 18, 18, 20, 20, 20, 20): Ch 1, hdc in next st, dec in next 2 sts, hdc across, turn. (12 [14, 16, 22, 22, 24, 22, 24, 24, 24] sts)

SHORT ROW SHAPING

Row 1 (RS): Ch 1, hdc across next 12 (14, 16, 22, 22, 24, 22, 24, 24, 24) sts, rotating work 90 degrees to work in ends of rows, sc in end of each of next 3 rows, turn. (12 [14, 16, 22, 22, 24, 22, 24, 24, 24] hdc, 3 sc)

Row 2: Ch 1, sk first sc, hdc in next 4 sts, 2 hdc in next st, place sm (see Pattern Notes) in st just made, hdc across, rotating work 90 degrees to work in ends of rows, sk 1 row end, sc in end of each of next 3 rows, turn.

Row 3: Ch 1, sk first sc, hdc in next 4 sts, 2 hdc in next st, place sm in st just made, hdc across, rotate work, sc in same row end as last sc worked 2 rows earlier, sc in each of next 2 row ends, turn.

Row 4: Ch 1, sk first sc, hdc across to marked st, 2 hdc in marked st, move sm to first of last 2 hdc made, hdc across, rotate work, sc in same row end as last sc worked 2 rows earlier, sc in each of next 2 row ends, turn.

Row 5: Ch 1, sk first sc, hdc across to marked st, 2 hdc in marked st, move sm to first of last 2 hdc made, hdc across, rotate work, sc in same row end as last sc worked 2 rows earlier, sc in each of next 2 row ends, turn.

Row 6: Ch 1, sk first sc, hdc across to marked st, 2 hdc in marked st, move sm to hdc just made, hdc across, rotate work, sc in same row end as last sc worked, sc in each of next 2 row ends, turn.

Row 7: Ch 1, sk first sc, hdc across to marked st, 2 hdc in marked st, move sm to hdc just made, hdc across, rotate work, sc in same row end as last sc worked, sc in each of next 2 row ends, turn.

Rep rows 4–7 until there are 36 (38, 49, 49, 51, 51, 57, 59, 59, 61) sts.

Next 7 rows: Ch 1, sk first sc, hdc across, rotate work, sc in same row end as last sc worked, sc in each of next 2 row ends. (50 [52, 63, 63, 65, 65, 71, 73, 73, 75] sts after 7th row) Fasten off.

COLLAR

Row 1: With RS of Front facing, join in first row edge at bottom left of front neck opening (this is the right-hand side of the garment when worn), ch 1, work 11 (13, 18, 18, 20, 20, 20, 22, 22, 24) sc evenly across front neck edge toward Hood, continue with hdc across all Hood sts, work 11 (13, 18, 18, 20, 20, 20, 22, 22, 24) sc evenly across opposite front neck edge toward bottom of neck opening. (72 [78, 99, 99, 105, 105, 111, 117, 117, 123] sts)

Rows 2–3: Ch 1, hdc across, turn.

Row 4: Ch 1, 11 (13, 18, 18, 20, 20, 20, 22, 22, 24) hdc, 2 hdc in next hdc, 48 (50, 61, 61, 63, 63, 69, 71, 71, 73) hdc, 2 hdc in next hdc, 11 (13, 18, 18, 20, 20, 20, 22, 22, 24) hdc, turn. (74 [80, 101, 101, 107, 107, 113, 119, 119, 125] sts)

Rows 5–10: Ch 1, hdc across, turn. Fasten off.

FINISHING

Overlap one edge of lower Collar over the other and sew edges to bottom of neck opening.

Sew Sleeve Cap into Armhole Opening.

Lay RS of Back on RS of Front Pocket and Front, with whip stitch, sew through all layers at lower side seams, then through 2 layers up to Sleeves, continue to sew Sleeve sides together.

Join in side seam to work across Front, ch 1. Working through both layers of Front and Front Pocket, sc evenly across to close bottom opening, then sc evenly across Back. Join in first sc. Fasten off.

Weave in all ends.

Soak in warm water with a half capful of gentle shampoo. Allow to soak until cold. Drain water. Without wringing, squeeze as much water out of hoodie as possible. Lay on several layers of towels and roll up. Squeeze out as much water as possible into towels. Remove hoodie from towel and lay flat. Stretch and pat until it matches the final measurements. Allow to air dry completely.

Toothy Grin, Small Pattern

Pattern is not to scale. Refer to instructions for Child-Size Emoji Chart on page 92. Colors shown correspond to yarn colors, except as shown below.

White squares not in mouth: Work with main color chosen for hoodie.

Yellow squares with diagonal mark: After working color changes, bottom of stitch is brown and top of same stitch is yellow.

White squares with diagonal mark: After working color changes, bottom of stitch is brown and top of same stitch is main color of hoodie.

Toothy Grin, Large Pattern

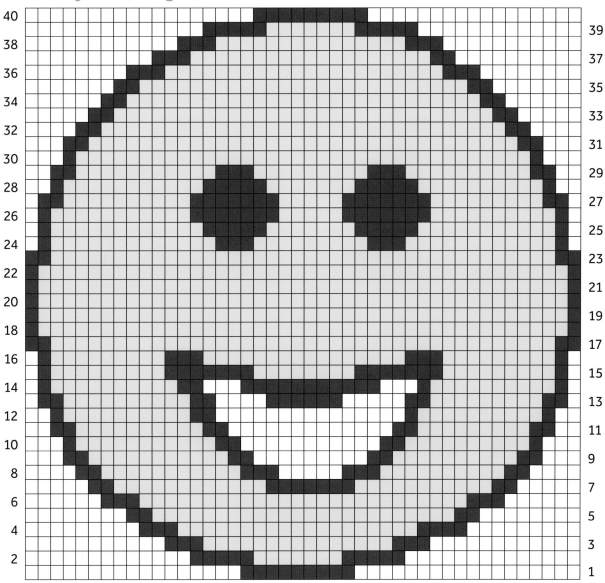

Pattern is not to scale. Refer to instructions for Adult-Size Emoji Chart on page 93.
Colors shown correspond to yarn colors, except as shown below.

White squares not in mouth: Work with main color chosen for hoodie.

Smile, Small Pattern

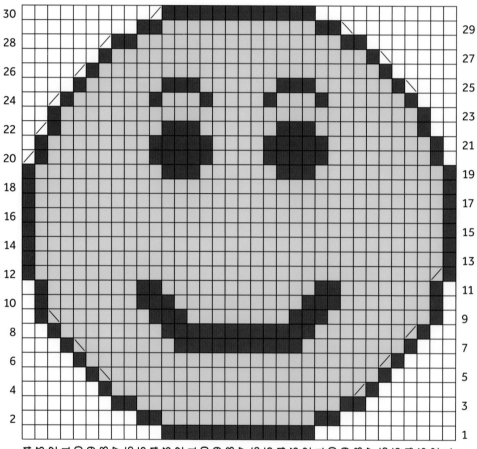

Pattern is not to scale. Colors shown correspond to yarn colors, except as shown below.

White squares: Work with main color chosen for hoodie.

Yellow squares with diagonal mark: After working color changes, bottom of stitch is brown and top of same stitch is yellow.

White squares with diagonal mark: After working color changes, bottom of stitch is brown and top of same stitch is main color of hoodie.

Smile, Large Pattern

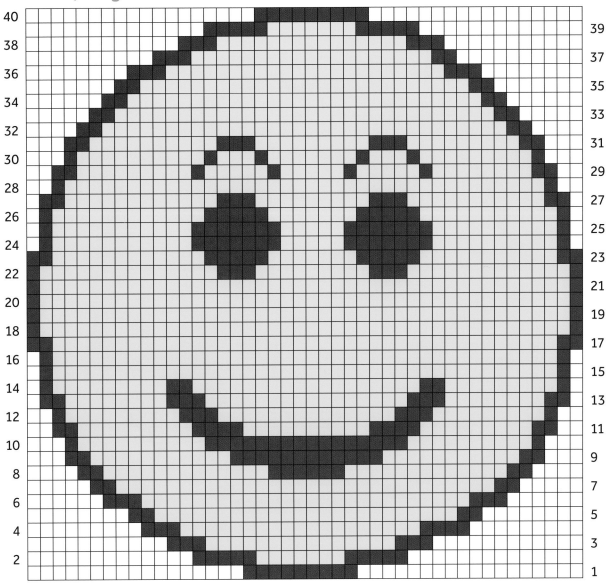

Pattern is not to scale. Colors shown correspond to yarn colors, except as shown below.

White squares: Work with main color chosen for hoodie.

Template, Small Pattern

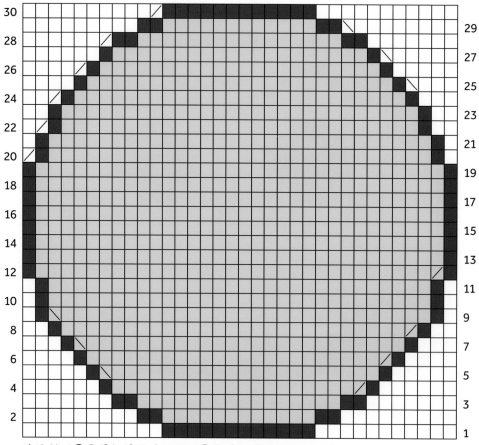

Pattern is not to scale. Colors shown correspond to yarn colors, except as shown below. Photocopy this template and fill in an emoji design of your choice.

White squares: Work with main color chosen for hoodie.

Yellow squares with diagonal mark: After working color changes, bottom of stitch is brown and top of same stitch is yellow.

White squares with diagonal mark: After working color changes, bottom of stitch is brown and top of same stitch is main color of hoodie.

Template, Large Pattern

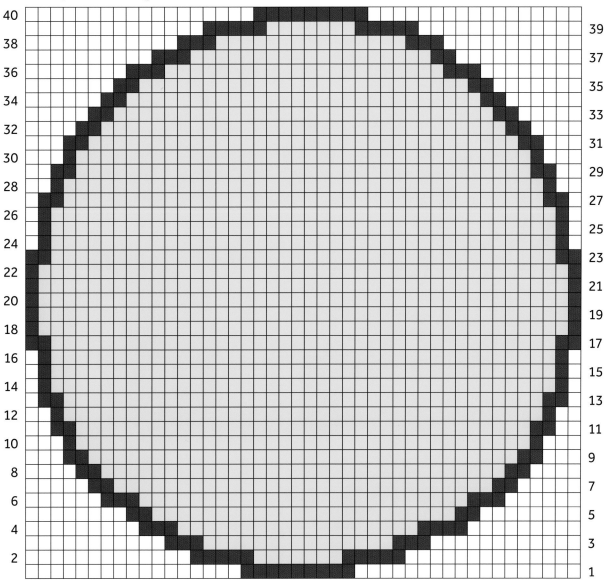

Pattern is not to scale. Colors shown correspond to yarn colors, except as shown below. Photocopy this template and fill in an emoji design of your choice.

White squares: Work with main color chosen for hoodie.

ACCESSORIES

At home or on the go, accessorize your life with these emoji projects. Express your inner nerd with the Brainac Bag (page 104), which is great for stashing your essential travel stuff. Craft the Striped Pencil Case (page 116) to accessorize your classwork, or crochet the Cool Guy Hacky Sack (page 119) to kick around with your friends after school. Bobble Head Earrings (page 107) will put a smile on anyone's face at home or away. And don't forget to bring emojis to your bathroom with the Sleepy Time Washcloth (page 110)!

BRAINIAC BAG

Nerdy and geeky is in! This shoulder bag celebrates young women who love to learn and love science and all things geek—but there's nothing stopping you from changing colors and using different emoji facial elements from page 16 to give this bag a different character.

FINISHED MEASUREMENTS
Diameter: 8 ¼ inches (21cm)
Width: 3 ½ inches (9cm)

GAUGE
Worked in the round, 19 sc =
4 inches (10cm); 17 rnds =
4 inches (10cm)
First 5 rnds of face circle =
2 ¼ inches (6cm) in diameter

LIGHT

MATERIALS + TOOLS

- DK weight yarn (55% acrylic, 45% cotton), 3.5 oz (100g) / 250 yds (229m) per ball, in the following colors:
  - 1 ball, lavender
  - 1 ball, navy blue
  - 1 ball, white
- 3.75mm hook or size needed to achieve gauge
- Locking stitch markers
- Matching sewing thread and needle
- Sharp tapestry needle
- 14-in. (35cm) plastic zipper

Note: Join with sl st unless otherwise indicated.

FACIAL FEATURES DIRECTORY

Use the facial elements from Crocheted Facial Features (page 16) to customize your emoji design. Just be sure to use yarn that is the same weight as the rest of your project to keep the face proportional.

Eyes: Eyes with Spectacles
Mouth: Mouth, Large
Other: Teeth

FACE CIRCLE

Make 2.

Rnd 1: With lavender, make 7 sc into adjustable ring, place sm in last st made. (7 sc)

Rnd 2: Continue working in spiral without joining at end of rnds, moving sm to last st worked in each rnd. 2sc in each st around. (14 sc)

Rnd 3: [1 sc, 2sc in next st] around. (21 sc)

Rnd 4: [2sc in next st, 2 sc] around. (28 sc)

Rnd 5: [3 sc, 2sc in next st] around. (35 sc)

Rnd 6: [1 sc, 2sc in next st, 3 sc] around. (42 sc)

Rnd 7: [2sc in next st, 5 sc] around. (49 sc)

Rnd 8: [3 sc, 2sc in next st, 3 sc] around. (56 sc)

Rnd 9: [2sc in next st, 7 sc] around. (63 sc)

Rnd 10: [4 sc, 2sc in next st, 4 sc] around. (70 sc)

Rnd 11: [2sc in next st, 9 sc] around. (77 sc)

Rnd 12: [5 sc, 2sc in next st, 5 sc] around. (84 sc)

Rnd 13: [13 sc, 2sc in next st] 6 times. (90 sc)

Rnd 14: [7 sc, 2sc in next st, 7 sc] around. (96 sc)

Rnd 15: [15 sc, 2sc in next st] around. (102 sc)

Rnd 16: [8 sc, 2sc in next st, 8sc] around. (108 sc)

Rnd 17: [17 sc, 2sc in next st] around, changing to navy blue in last yo, and pull through last sc. (114 sc)

Rnd 18: With navy blue, [9 hdc, 2hdc in next st, 9 hdc] around, sl st in first hdc. (120 hdc)

Rnd 19: Ch 1, working in lower back bar of each st around, [15 sc, dec] 7 times, sc in last st, changing to lavender with last yo and pull through, join in first sc. (113 sts)

Rnds 20–27: Ch 1, sc in each st around, join in first sc. End with sewn invisible join (see page 13).

FACIAL FEATURES

Create faces using the Facial Features instructions starting on page 16. Mix and match as desired. If you wish to create the faces shown in the photographed project, consult the grid at left.

ASSEMBLY

Weave in all ends.

Sew plastic zipper to corresponding sides of Face Circle edges. Place facial features so top of face aligns with zipper and sew in place with matching thread. With yarn and tapestry needle and RS tog, sew remaining bag seam with whip stitch.

STRAP

Row 1: Ch 21, sc in 2nd ch from hook and in each ch across, turn. (20 sc)

Row 2: Ch 1, sc in each st across, turn.

Rep row 2 until Strap measures 4 feet (1.2m) or desired length. Fasten off.

Sew strap to bag on either side of zipper ends with matching thread.

BOBBLE HEAD EARRINGS

Crocheting small tiny things is fun and quick. These emoji earrings are a great introduction to crocheting with cotton thread if you haven't tried it before. Size 10 cotton isn't the thinnest you can go, so if you want to make them even tinier, there are smaller hooks and threads available. You could also make 20 or so of these little emoji heads and string them together for a bracelet or necklace.

FINISHED MEASUREMENTS
Diameter: ⅝-inch (16mm)

GAUGE
Not essential for this project. Tighter is better.

MATERIALS + TOOLS

- Lace weight thread (100% mercerized cotton), 0.87 oz (25g) / 122 yds (112m) per ball, in the following colors:
  - 1 ball, green
  - 1 ball, pink
- 1.25mm steel crochet hook
- #6 seed beads for filling
- 2 soldered jump rings
- 2 leverback earring settings
- Upholstery needle

SPECIAL STITCHES

Increase (inc): 2 sc worked into same st.

Decrease (dec): Insert hook in front lp of next st, yo, pull up lp, insert hook in back lp of next st, yo, pull through all lps on hook.

EARRING

Rnd 1: With green, 6 sc in adjustable ring. Do not join, continue following rnds without joining. (6 sc)

Rnd 2: Inc (see Special Stitches) in each st around. (12 sc)

Rnd 3: [1 sc, inc] 6 times. (18 sc)

Rnd 4: 1 sc, inc, 1 sc, inc. With pink, 2 sc, inc, 4 sc. With green, 1 sc in same st as last, [2 sc, inc] twice, 1 sc. (24 sts)

Rnd 5: 2 sc, inc, 3 sc. With pink, inc. With green, 6 sc in blo. With pink, 2 sc. With green, 2 sc, inc, 6 sc. (27 sts)

Rnd 6: 2 sc, dec (see Special Stitches), 17 sc, dec, 4 sc. (25 sts)

Rnd 7: 10 sc. With pink, 1 sc. With green, 3 sc. With pink, 1 sc in same st as last. With green, 5 sc, dec, 5 sc. (25 sts)

Rnd 8: 4 sc, dec, 4 sc. With pink, 2 sc. With green, 1 sc, inc. With pink, 2 sc. With green, 4 sc, dec, 3 sc. (24 sts)

Rnd 9: [1 sc, dec, 1 sc] twice, 4 sc, dec, 2 sc, dec, 1 sc, dec, 1 sc, dec. (18 sts)

Rnd 10: [1 sc, dec] 6 times. (12 sts)

Other than working yarn, trim all ends to ½-inch (12mm) and stuff inside. Fill with as many beads as possible.

Rnd 11: [1 sc, sk 1] around until closed.

FINISHING

With upholstery needle, weave in through front lps of 3 or 4 sts and cinch hole closed.

Attach to jump rings; attach jump rings to small link in leverback earring fixings.

SLEEPY TIME WASHCLOTH

One of the most soothing parts of the bedtime routine when our boys were little was the bath. Other than the great time splashing around and playing with floating toys, they loved the soft cloths we used to wash their faces. This memory is what inspired the design of this washcloth. Change things up with several other faces, or draw your own with the template on page 115.

FINISHED MEASUREMENTS
12 ½ inches (32cm) square

GAUGE
17 hdc and 11 hdc rows = 4 inches (10cm)

MATERIALS + TOOLS

- DK weight yarn (100% cotton), 3.5 oz (100g) / 230 yds (210m) per ball, in the following colors:
  - 1 ball, lime green
  - 1 ball, black
  - 1 ball, yellow
- Size 4mm hook or size needed to achieve gauge
- Bobbins
- Sharp tapestry needle

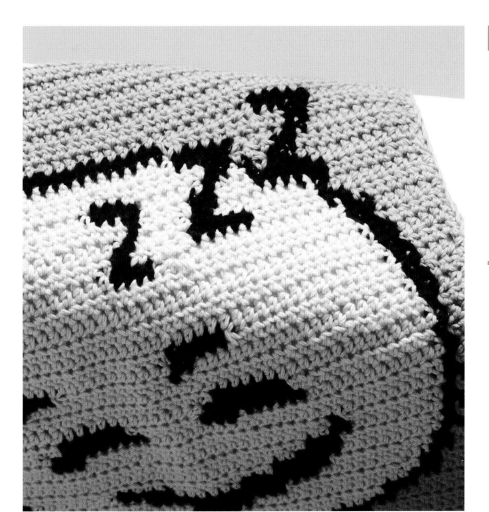

Note: Join with sl st unless otherwise indicated.

PATTERN NOTES

- To work crochet intarsia, you'll need to wind several meters of accent colors to create the face edging and the facial features. Prepare 4 bobbins with black yarn, 2 very full bobbins with yellow, and 1 bobbin with lime green. For the eyebrows, it's okay to use 6 ½ feet (2m) of black yarn without a bobbin and just pull the ends through to keep the bobbins from twisting.

- To work a reversible washcloth, there are several techniques you need to keep in mind as you work through the chart. Odd rows are read from right to left and even rows from left to right.

- To add a new color, work the hdc to the point where you have 3 lps on the hook. Yarn over in the new color (leaving a 4-inch [10cm] tail) and pull through all 3 lps on the hook; work the next st in the new color.

- When you have 1 to 4 sts that you need to work in a new color, but the yarn is several sts further forward from your current spot, drape the yarn loosely over the top of the sts and cover the draped yarn with the next sts.

- When you will need a color within a few sts from where you are, but the new color is at your current spot, trap the new color yarn under the next few sts worked in the current color.

- To change colors, work the current color to the point where you have 3 lps on the hook; yarn over in the new color, and draw through, bring the whole bobbin or skein of yarn from the back to the side of the work facing you and make sure the strand of old color yarn goes between the hook and the strand of new color yarn that you will use to make the next st. At the end of a row, all strands of yarn should be on the side facing you before you turn. If you've left a strand of yarn on the wrong side of the work, you'll need to undo your sts to that point and bring it forward. After you turn your work, all the strands will be on the side facing away from you to begin the new row. Untwist your bobbins every second row.

BOTTOM OF FRAME

Row 1: With lime green, ch 56, hdc in back ridge of 2nd ch from hook, hdc in back ridge of each ch across, turn. (55 hdc)

Rows 2–7: Ch 1 loosely, hdc in each st across, turn.

CHART

Row 1: Ch 1 loosely, following chart from right to left, work 19 hdc, work 20th hdc until there are 3 lps on hook, leaving a 4-inch (10cm) tail, join black with a yo and pull through 3 lps, bring lime green yarn forward between hook and black yarn, 13 hdc in black, work 14th hdc until there are 3 lps on hook, leaving a 4-inch (10cm) tail, join next bobbin of lime green with a yo and pull through 3 lps, bring black yarn forward between hook and lime green yarn, 21 hdc, turn.

Row 2: Ch 1 loosely, following chart from left to right, work 16, work 17th hdc until there are 3 lps on hook, bring black yarn up, yo, and pull through, bring lime green yarn forward between hook and black yarn, work 4 black hdc trapping the strand of black between the hdc and the top of the green stitches, in last hdc, change to yellow in the last yo, and pull through, bring black yarn forward between the hook and yellow yarn, work 14 hdc in yellow, in last hdc, yo and pull through last 3 lps with black, bring yellow forward between hook and black yarn, work 4 hdc in black, changing to lime green in last one, bring black forward between hook and lime green yarn, work rem sts in lime green.

Continue following chart rows 3–32 using techniques from Pattern Notes for color changes as established.

TOP OF FRAME

With lime green work 7 rows in even hdc. Do not fasten off.

EDGE

With lime green, ch 1, rotate work to continue down side of washcloth working in row ends, make 54 sc evenly across side, work 2 sc in corner, [work 54 sc evenly across next edge, 2 sc in corner] 3 times. Join in first sc. Fasten off.

Weave in ends by piercing through stitches and yarn strands with sharp tapestry needle. Work through and under 3 or 4 sts in one direction, then double back and weave through and under 2 or 3 sts in the opposite direction to secure.

Sleepy Time Pattern

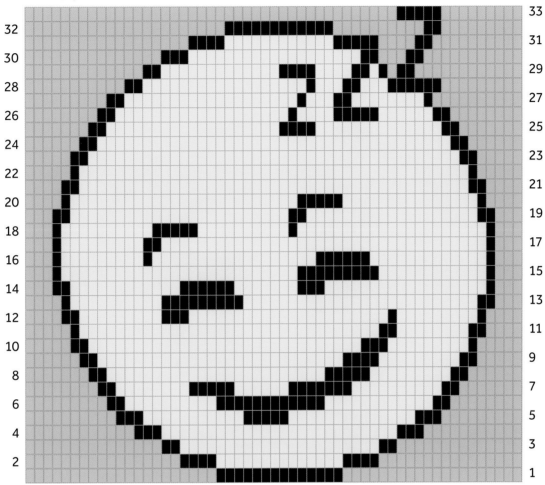

Pattern is not to scale. Refer to instructions for Pattern Notes and Chart on page 112.
Colors shown correspond to yarn colors.

Grin Pattern

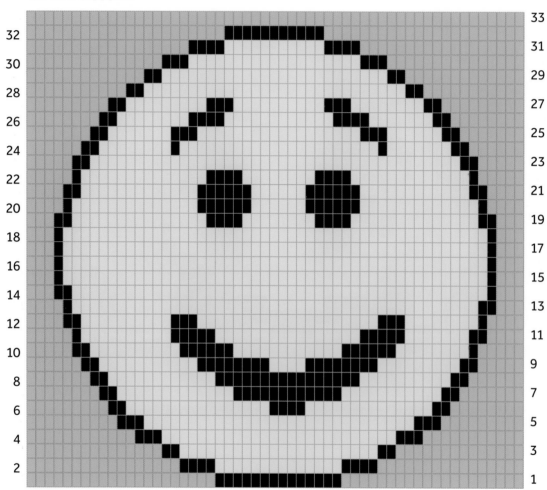

Pattern is not to scale. Refer to instructions for Pattern Notes on page 112.
Colors shown correspond to yarn colors.

Template Pattern

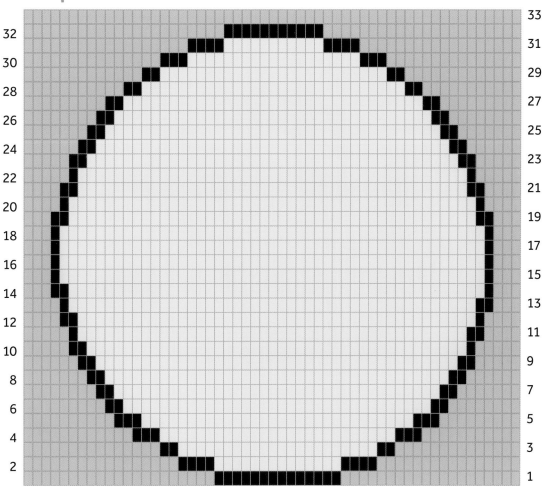

Pattern is not to scale. Refer to instructions for Pattern Notes on page 112.
Colors shown correspond to yarn colors. Photocopy this template and
fill in an emoji design of your choice.

STRIPED PENCIL CASE

Need a case for your pencils or a place to store your spare crochet hooks? This little zipped up case is the perfect pouch to store those tools. If you want to customize it, you can crochet the end faces without a contrasting color and appliqué on some emoji facial elements from page 16 instead. Use a durable cotton yarn and tight stitches to keep your treasures secure in the case.

FINISHED MEASUREMENTS
Length: 9 inches (25cm)
Around: 5 inches (12cm)

GAUGE
Worked in the round, 26 sc = 4 inches (10cm); 28 rounds = 4 inches (10cm)

MATERIALS + TOOLS

- Fingering weight yarn (100% mercerized cotton), 1.75oz (50g) / 136 yds (125m) per ball, in the following colors:
    - 1 ball, gray
    - 1 ball, teal
    - 1 ball, red
- 2.75mm hook or size necessary to achieve gauge
- 6 or 8-in. (15 or 20cm) zipper
- Sewing needle and matching sewing thread

SPECIAL STITCHES

Slip stitch 2 together (slst2tog): This st is worked on the WS of the work. Ch 1, insert hook in first st and draw up a lp, insert st in 2nd st, yo, and pull through all lps on hook, *insert hook in same st as last st worked and pull up a lp, insert hook in next st, yo and pull through all lps on hook; rep from * across, ending with sc in same st as last worked.

Note: Join with sl st unless otherwise indicated.

PATTERN NOTES

- To change to a new color, work last sc in prev color until there are 2 lps on the hook, yo with new color, pull through both lps on hook.

FACE

Rnd 1: With gray, make adjustable lp and ch 1, 6 sc in lp, join to first sc.

Rnd 2: Ch 1, 3sc in first st, 2sc in each of next 3 sts, sc in next st, 2sc in sl st, join in first sc. (10 sts)

When a color isn't in use, work sts over unused strand to trap it on top of next sts.

Rnd 3: Ch 1, sc in same st as join, 2sc in next st, change to teal (see Pattern Notes), 1 sc in teal, 2sc in next st in gray, 1 sc, (1 sc in teal, 1 sc in gray) in next st, [in gray, 1 sc, 2sc in next st] twice, 2 sc, sc in sl sp, join in first sc. (18 sts)

Rnd 4: Ch 1, sc in same st as join, 1 sc, 2sc in next st, 1 sc in teal, 2sc in next st in teal, 2 sc in gray, 2sc in next st in teal, 1 sc, [with gray, 2 sc, 2sc in next st] 3 times, join in first sc. (24 sts)

Rnd 5: Ch 1, sc in same st as join, 2 sc, 2sc in next st, 2sc in next st with teal, 2 sc, 1 sc with gray, 2sc in next st, 2 sc with teal, 2sc in next st, 4 sc with gray, 2sc in next st, [3 sc, 2sc in next st] twice, join in first sc. (32 sts)

Rnd 6: Ch 1, 3 sc, 2sc in next st, 2 sc, 2 sc in teal, 2sc in next st, 1 sc in gray, 2sc in next st, 1 sc, 4 sc in teal, 2 sc in gray, 2sc in st, 6 sc, 2sc in next st, 4 sc, 2sc in next st, 1 sc, join in first sc. (38 sts)

Rnd 7: Ch 1, 8 sc, 1 sc in teal, sk 1 st, 2 sc, 3 sc in gray, 2sc in next st, 2 sc in teal, sk 1 st, 1 sc, 1 sc in gray, 2sc in next st, 2 sc, [in teal, 1 sc, 2sc in next st] 6 times, 2 sc in next st, 2sc in next st in gray, join to first sc. (46 sts)

Rnd 8: In gray, ch 1, sc in same st as join, 4 sc, [2sc in next st, 5 sc] 7 times, 1 sc, join in first sc. (55 sts)

Rnd 9: Ch 1, sc in same st as join, [9 sc, 2sc in next st] 5 times, 3 sc, join in first sc. (59 sts)

Rnd 10: Ch 1, hdc in same st as join, 58 hdc, join in blo of first hdc. (59 hdc)

SIDES

Rnd 11: Ch 1, roll top edge of hdc toward you to see the 3rd back strand of each hdc, sc in back strand of each hdc around, work sewn invisible join (see page 13).

Rnd 12: With red, join in the st that lands at the top of the face between the 2 eyes, ch 1, sc in same st, sc in each st around, join in first sc, turn.

Rnd 13: Ch 1, sc in each st around, join in first sc, turn.

Rep rnd 13 with red or with random teal stripes to taste until work measures 1½ inches (38mm) from lip formed in rnd 11.

OPENING

Now working in rows.

Row 14: Ch 1, sc in each st around. Do not join, turn.

Row 15: Ch 1, sc in each st around, turn.

Rep row 15, with random red and teal stripes to taste until work measures 4 inches (10cm) from lip ending with a WS row.

STRENGTHENING BAND

Row 16: Ch 1, 5 sc, [2sc in next st, 10 sc] 3 times, sc in each rem st, changing to gray in last st, turn. (62 sts)

Row 17: Ch 1, work slst2tog (see Special Stitches) across, sc in same st as last sl st, turn.

Row 18: Ch 1, sc in blo across, turn.

Rep rows 17–18 until Strengthening Band is approximately 1 inch (25mm) wide, changing to red in last st, turn.

Next row: Ch 1, 3 sc, [sk next st, 11 sc] 3 times, sc in each rem st, turn. (59 sts)

Rep row 15 with random red and teal stripes to taste until work from split for opening measures length of zipper (6 or 8 inches [15 or 20cm]).

Rep row 13 twice. Fasten off.

OPPOSITE END

Rep instructions from beginning of Face to rnd 13. Rep rnd 13 if necessary to make 2nd end of case the same length to the split as the first end. Fasten off.

ASSEMBLY

Turn pieces inside out. Holding RS together, sew ends together with whip stitch seam.

Weave in all ends.

Sew in zipper with matching thread and sewing needle.

COOL GUY HACKY SACK

This little guy can be used for the fun game of hacky sack, or make several of them to use as juggling balls. If you fill them with metal beads, they make perfect paper weights. Another option is to fill the bottom with metal beads and the top with a polyester filler—now you have a pin cushion.

FINISHED MEASUREMENTS

Height: 2 ½ inches (7cm)
Around: 7 inches (18cm)

GAUGE

Worked in the round,
24 sc = 4 inches (10cm);
26 rows = 4 inches

LIGHT

MATERIALS + TOOLS

- Fingering weight yarn (100% mercerized cotton), 1.75oz (50g) / 136 yds (125m) per ball, in the following colors:
  - 1 ball, yellow
  - 1 ball, blue
- Filler (pellets, sand, rice, pearl barley, #6 plastic beads)
- 3.25mm hook or size necessary to achieve gauge
- Locking stitch marker

SPECIAL STITCHES

Decrease (dec): Insert hook in back lp of next st, yo, pull up lp, insert hook in front lp of next st, yo, pull yarn through all lps on hook.

ADJUSTABLE RING

Rnd 1: In yellow, 6 sc into ring, place sm into last sc made, move sm up.

Rnd 2: 2sc into each st around. (12 sc)

Rnd 3: [1 sc, 2sc in next st] around. (18 sc)

Rnd 4: [5 sc, 2sc in next st] around. (21 sc)

Rnd 5: [2 sc, 2sc in next st] around. (28 sc)

Rnd 6: [3 sc, 2sc in next st] 6 times, 4 sc. (34 sc)

Rnd 7: [7 sc, 2sc in next st] 4 times, 2 sc. (38 sc)

Rnd 8: [11 sc, 2sc in next st] 3 times, 2 sc. (41 sc)

Rnd 9: 1 sc, 2sc in next st, 3 sc, 1 sc and change to blue, 8 sc, 1 sc and change to yellow, 6 sc, 2sc in next st, 19 sc. (43 sc)

Rnd 10: 3 sc, 1 sc and change to blue, 15 sc, 1 sc and change to yellow, 10 sc, 2sc in next st, 12 sc. (44 sc)

Rnd 11: 3 sc, 1 sc and change to blue, 1 sc, 1 sc and change to yellow, 12 sc (catching blue strand under every other st), 1 sc and change to blue, 1 sc, 1 sc and change to blue, 12 sc, 2sc in next st, 10 sc. (45 sc)

Rnds 12–16: Sc with yellow around.

Rnd 17: 8 sc, 1 sc and change to blue, 2 sc, 1 sc and change to yellow, 3 sc, 1 sc and change to blue, 2 sc, 1 sc and change to yellow, 8 sc, dec, 16 sc. (44 sc)

Rnd 18: 8 sc, 1 sc and change to blue, 3 sc, 1 sc and change to yellow, 2 sc, 1 sc and change to blue, 3 sc, 1 sc and change to yellow, 11 sc, dec, 11 sc. (43 sc)

Rnd 19: Dec, 5 sc, 1 sc and change to blue, 4 sc, 1 sc and change to yellow, 1 sc, 1 sc and change to blue, 4 sc, 1 sc and change to yellow, 7 sc, dec, 14 sc. (41 sc)

Rnd 20: 2 sc, dec, 2 sc, 1 sc and change to blue, 12 sc, 1 sc and change to yellow, 5 sc, dec, 6 sc, dec, 6 sc. (38 sc)

Turn inside out and weave in ends, then turn right side out.

Rnd 21: 4 sc, [dec, 7 sc] 3 times, dec, 5 sc. (34 sc)

Rnd 22: [Dec, 3 sc] 6 times, 4 sc. (28 sc)

Rnd 23: [2 sc, dec] 7 times. (21 sc)

Rnd 24: [5 sc, dec] 3 times. (18 sc)

Fill with desired filler.

Rnd 25: [1 sc, dec] 6 times. (12 sc)

Rnd 26: [Dec] 6 times. (6 sc) Fasten off.

With tapestry needle, weave in end under front lp of each of 6 sts and cinch closed tightly. Weave in end.

PROJECT COLORS

The projects in this book were made using the yarn brands and colors outlined below. Feel free to use your favorite brand of appropriate weight yarn (available online and through your local yarn shop).

HOME DECOR

25'S A CROWD BLANKET
 Cascade Yarns North Shore (100% acrylic), 3.5 oz (100g) / 220 yds (200m) per ball, in 18 Daffodil, 09 Black, 29 Chrysanthemum, 10 Red, 03 Sapphire, 19 Grasshopper, 24 Cherry, 04 Violet, 22 Teal

STINKY FEET OTTOMAN
 Patons Shetland Chunky (100% acrylic), 3.5 oz (100g) / 148 yds (136m) per ball, in 78526 Leaf Green, 78040 Black, 78006 White

CHILLIN' OUT CUSHION
 Caron Simply Soft (100% acrylic), 6 oz (170g) / 315 yds (288m) per ball, in 9770 Cool Green, 9727 Black, 9779 Green, 0014 Pagoda

SWEET STUFF CUSHION
 Bernat Softee Baby (100% acrylic), 5 oz (140g) / 362 yds (331m) per ball, in 30205 Prettiest Pink, 30424 Soft Red, 30111 Blue Jeans

TAUNTING MEGA CUSHION
 Bernat Satin (100% acrylic), 3.5 oz (100g) / 200yds (180m) per ball, in 4615 Banana, 4221 Soft Fern, 4203 Teal, 4040 Ebony, 4705 Crimson, 4307 Sultana

9 FACES LAPGHAN
 Caron Simply Soft (100% acrylic), 6 oz (170 g) / 315 yds (288m) per ball, in 9722 Plum Wine, 9717 Orchid, 0005 Blackberry, 9709 Light Country Blue, 9721 Victorian Rose, 0015 Strawberry, 9737 Light Country Peach, 9755 Sunshine

CLOTHES

BABY BEANIES
 Kraemer Yarns Perfection (70% acrylic, 30% merino wool), 3.5 oz (100g) / 260 yds (238m) per ball, in 2273 Blueberry Buckle, 2240 Onyx, 2243 Coral Belle, 2261 Snowflake

NUM NUM BIB
 Cascade Yarns North Shore (100% acrylic), 3.5 oz (100g) / 220 yds (200m) per ball, in 21 Aqua, 17 Lemon Sorbet, 08 Silver, 29 Chrysanthemum

SURLY SLOUCHIE HAT
 Kraemer Yarns Perfection (70% acrylic, 30% merino wool), 3.5 oz (100g) / 260 yds (238m) per ball, in 2255 Flame Red, 2256 Orange, 2240 Onyx

POM-POM BEANIE
 Cascade Yarns Cherub Chunky (55% nylon, 45% acrylic), 3.5 oz (100g) / 137 yds (125m) per ball, in 14 Melon, 40 Black, 25 Ruby

KISSY POCKET SCARF
 Patons Astra (100% acrylic), 1.75 oz (50g) / 161 yds (147m) per ball, in 02941 School Bus Yellow, 02765 Black, 08436 Cherry, 02751 White, 02733 Electric Blue, 08417 Peony Pink

NOT TOO BLUE FOR YOU MITTENS
 or Cascade Yarns 220 Superwash Effects (100% superwash wool), 3.5 oz (100g) / 220 yds (200m) per ball, in 06 Stormy Sea; Cascade Yarns 220 in 904 Colonial Blue Heather, 885 In the Navy

SMELLY SLIPPERS
 Bernat Super Value (100% acrylic), 7 oz (197g) / 275 yds (251m) per ball, in 0608 Bright Yellow, 0609 Kelly Green, 7421 Black, 0607 Berry

BIG GRIN HOODIE
 Universal Yarn Adore (55% superwash merino wool/ 45% acrylic), 3.5 oz (100g) / 273 yds (250m) per ball, in 111 Banana, 119 Emerald, 127 Hickory, 104 Powder

ACCESSORIES

BRAINIAC BAG

 Kraemer Yarns Tatamy (55% acrylic, 45% cotton), 3.5 oz (100g) / 250 yds (229m) per ball, in 1728 Navy, 1736 Pearl, 1704 Sleepyhead

BOBBLE HEAD EARRINGS

 Handy Hands Lizbeth size 10 (100% mercerized cotton), 0.87 oz (25g) / 122 yds (112m) per ball, in 677 Lime Green Medium, 628 Salmon Medium

SLEEPY TIME WASHCLOTH

 Universal Yarn Cotton Supreme (100% cotton), 3.5 oz (100g) / 230 yds (210m) per ball, in 707 Yellow, 709 Lime, 718 Black

STRIPED PENCIL CASE

 Patons Grace (100% mercerized cotton), 1.75oz (50g) / 136 yds (125m) per ball, in 62044 Clay, 62705 Cardinal, 62201 Peacock

COOL GUY HACKY SACK

 Patons Grace (100% mercerized cotton), 1.75oz (50g) / 136 yds (125m) per ball, in 62622 Sunkissed, 62104 Azure

CROCHET ABBREVIATIONS

( )	work instructions within a pair of parentheses into the same insertion point
( )	separates different sizes of the same project
[ ]	work instructions within brackets as many times as directed
*	repeat the instructions following the single asterisk as directed
* *	repeat instructions between asterisks as many times as directed or repeat from a given set of instructions
approx	approximately
bdec	blended decrease
beg	begin/beginning
bet	between
blo	back loop(s) only
bsc	backward single cochet
ch	chain stitch
ch-	refers to chain or space previously made: e.g., ch-1 space
ch-sp(s)	chain space(s)
dc	double crochet
dc2tog	double crochet 2 stitches together
dec	decrease(s)/decreasing
e-sc	extended single crochet
fdc	foundation double crochet
fhdc	foundation half-double crochet

flo	front loop only
fsc	foundation single crochet
hdc	half-double crochet
hhdc	herringbone half-double crochet
inc	increase
invdec	invisible decrease
ldc	linked double crochet
lp(s)	loops
pm	place marker
prev	previous
rem	remain/remaining
rep	repeat(s)/repeating
rnd(s)	round(s)
RS	right side
sc	single crochet
sc2tog	single crochet 2 stitches together
sk	skip
slst2tog	slip stitch 2 together
sl st	slip stitch
sl-st-cl	slip stitch cluster
sm	stitch marker
split sc	split single crochet
sp(s)	space(s)
sslst	surface slip stitch
st(s)	stitch(es)
tr	treble crochet
tog	together
WS	wrong side
yo	yarn over

CROCHET HOOK SIZES

Millimeter	U.S. Size*
2.25mm	B-1
2.75mm	C-2
3.25mm	D-3
3.5mm	E-4
3.75mm	F-5
4mm	G-6
4.5mm	7
5mm	H-8
5.5mm	I-9
6mm	J-10
6.5mm	K-10½
8mm	L-11
9mm	M/N-13

*Letter or number may vary. Rely on the millimeter sizing.

YARN WEIGHT CHART

Yarn Weight Symbol & Category Names	0 LACE	1 SUPER FINE	2 FINE	3 LIGHT	4 MEDIUM	5 BULKY	6 SUPER BULKY	7 JUMBO
Types of Yarns in Category	Fingering, 10 count crochet thread	Sock, Fingering, Baby	Sport, Baby	DK, Light Worsted	Worsted, Afghan, Aran	Chucky, Craft, Rug	Bulky, Roving	Jumbo, Roving

Source: Craft Yarn Council's www.YarnStandards.com

BLANK GRIDS TO MAKE YOUR OWN PICTURE CHARTS

With these grids, you can do more than make your own emoji faces. You can transform any picture into a chart to crochet from. It's best to use pictures that have thick lines and less than ten colors so that it doesn't get too challenging to keep all those bobbins straight. The height and width of a crochet stitch are never equal to each other, so making charts using regular grid paper actually makes your finished crochet project look squat. The thickness of the yarn also affects stitch size quite a bit, so these grids will work best for worsted-weight and DK-weight yarns. The best way to use these grids is to photocopy or scan them to print them onto overhead transparency acetate sheets. Then you can place the transparency over your picture, color with erasable markers, and re-use the grids to your heart's content.

55 x 55-Block Grid to Use with All Half-Double Crochet Stitches

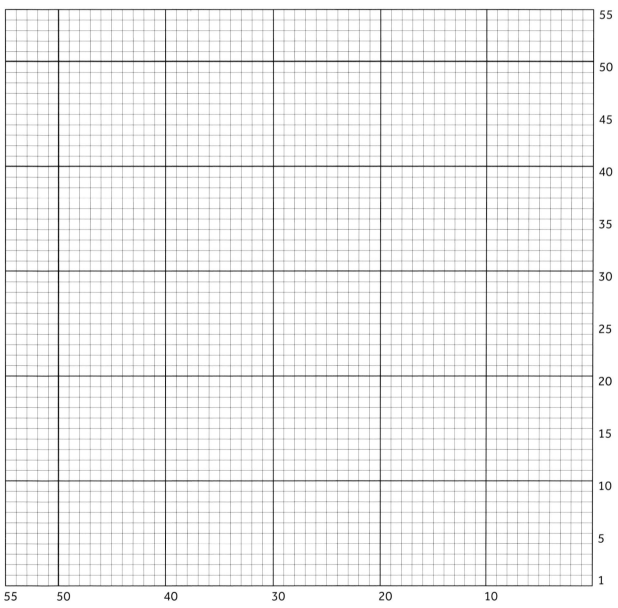

70 x 80-Block Grid to Use with All Single Crochet Stitches

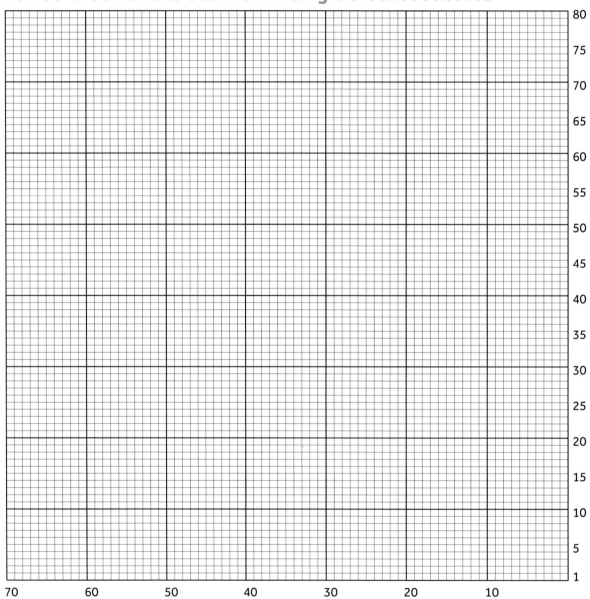

INDEX

Small Hexagon Puff Stitch Grid

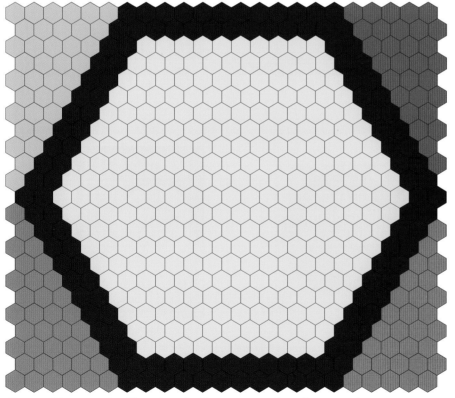

This small hexagonal puff stitch grid will give you crocheted squares that are 16 inches (41cm) square to make a smaller version of the throw cushion with whichever emoji face you'd like to color onto the grid yourself. To see how to make these puff stitch rows, go to page 44 and follow the bobble stitch pattern and color changing instructions. You will start with 58 foundation single crochet stitches.

MORE GREAT BOOKS *from*
SPRING HOUSE PRESS

Crochet Baskets
978-1940611-61-7
$22.95 | 128 Pages

Christmas Ornaments to Crochet
978-1940611-48-8
$22.95 | 136 Pages

Construction Vehicles to Crochet
978-1-940611-57-0
$22.95 | 128 Pages

The Natural Beauty Solution
ISBN: 978-1-940611-18-1
$19.95 | 128 Pages

Fabulous Fat Quarter Aprons
978-1-940611-39-6
$12.99 | 56 Pages

**Weighted Blankets,
Vests, and Scarves**
978-1940611-46-4
$12.99 | 48 Pages

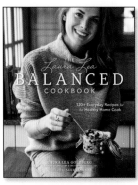

**The Laura Lea
Balanced Cookbook**
978-1-940611-56-3
$30.00 | 368 Pages

**A Colander, Cake Stand, and My
Grandfather's Iron Skillet**
978-1-940611-36-5
$24.95 | 184 Pages

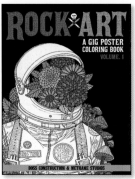

**Rock Art:
The Gig Poster Coloring Book**
978-1940611-42-6
$12.99 | 80 Pages

SPRING HOUSE PRESS

Look for these Spring House Press titles at your favorite bookstore, specialty retailer, or visit *www.springhousepress.com*.
For more information about Spring House Press, call 717-208-3739 or email us at *info@springhousepress.com*.